CHRISTIANS
IN THE
MARKETPLACE
BILL HYBELS

VICTOR BOOKS

A DIVISION OF SCRIPTURE PRESS PUBLICATIONS INC.
USA CANADA ENGLAND

Scripture quotations are from the *New American Standard Bible,* ©
the Lockman Foundation 1960, 1962, 1963, 1968, 1971, 1972, 1973,
1975, 1977. Used by permission.

Recommended Dewey Decimal Classification: 248.4
Suggested Subject Heading: PROFESSIONAL GROWTH
Library of Congress Catalog Card Number: 82-50135
ISBN: 0-89693-073-4

11 12 13 14 15 16 17 18 19 20 Printing/Year 96 95 94 93 92

Contents

Dedication

I dedicate this book to my father, Harold Hybels, who taught me the value of diligent labor; to my wife, Lynne, who exemplified it as she skillfully arranged the words of my Sunday messages into a form suitable for publication; and to the members of my congregation, both those who helped directly, as they typed and retyped the manuscript, and those who helped indirectly, as they "fleshed-out" and tested the principles set forth in this book in their real-life marketplaces.

The Marketplace: a Challenge (Preface)

Why is a minister talking about the "marketplace"? Shouldn't he be speaking to religious issues as ministers of the Gospel have been doing for hundreds of years? What interest, if any, does God have in the marketplace? Does He really know that it exists? Does He know what goes on there? Does He care? Didn't He design the church as a refuge from the marketplace?

These questions are typical, and because of them many Christian leaders have avoided the subject of the marketplace. And yet, one of the greatest challenges facing the true follower of Jesus Christ lies in determining how he or she should fit into the marketplace of the world. Should not then the church address itself to this subject?

It is in the workplace that most people (Christians included) spend the majority of their time. How do Christian believers fit into that world? How should the Christian view his or her work? How should he behave there? Should he enjoy his profession or merely endure it? Should the sincere follower of Christ leave the marketplace and enter "full-time Christian work" as a sign of his maturity and deep-level commitment? Is a believer ever justified in allowing his job to interfere with his spiritual growth? Is it ethical for the Christian to view his workplace simply as one more area to evangelize? Can there be a truly Christian businessman or businesswoman? Does the Bible answer these questions?

I have seen in my own church that as men and women receive Christ as their Saviour and then slowly learn to follow Him as Lord, they become increasingly aware that Christianity is a day-by-day, moment-by-moment walk with the Lord. It affects their values, personalities, relationships, vocabularies, marriages, work—in short, every area of their lives. True believers cannot compartmentalize their lives. They cannot go to church and Bible studies and other "Christian activities" wearing sanctified masks of godliness,

7

and then trade them for the more comfortable masks of worldliness as they enter the marketplace. No, true Christians cannot do that. Because the Holy Spirit lives within them, wherever they go they take with them minds that have been renewed and attitudes that are being conformed to the attitudes of Christ. When the true Christian enters the marketplace, Christ enters with him, and together they must leave there a mark of holiness.

It is to that end that this book is dedicated.

One

Human Labor: Necessary Evil, Or God's Design?

"I want to buy a new car, pay off my house, quit my job, and *never work again!*" So goes the typical response of a recent lottery winner or recipient of a generous inheritance. *I'm never going to work again! I can rid myself of the curse of mankind! I'll be free!* I wonder how many people would like to echo those words and cast off the chains of labor.

Work seems to have risen to the status of the number one necessary evil in this country. The average person endures the weekly grind only by relishing the anticipation of the workless weekend; and nearly everyone plans for an early retirement. Even Christians share this view. They believe that labor came about by default, rather than by the design of God. They envision God screaming at Adam and Eve in relentless anger: "You despicable sinners. There's only one thing horrible enough to be a fitting punishment for your disobedience. You shall work! Work! Work!" The picture of human labor is painted with sadistic, vengeful strokes.

Is that how God would have us view labor—as the dreadful punishment due fallen man? Genesis 1 paints the first picture of labor. We read that "God created . . . and God was moving . . . and God separated . . . and God called . . . and God made . . . and God gathered . . . and God placed . . . and God blessed." Step by step, day by day, God labored over Creation. The labor was not His curse, His punishment. It was His choice. He willfully, voluntarily, and joyfully brought this world into existence, and when He finished and studied His Creation He said, "Yes, this is *very good.*" The result of His skillful work brought Him joy and a tremendous sense of accomplishment.

The next biblical picture of labor is in Genesis 2, where God told Adam to cultivate and care for the Garden of Eden. Adam had not yet sinned, so surely there could be no vengeance in this command. On the contrary, God was saying, "Adam, I love you. I've already given you time, and now I choose to give you something precious and worthwhile to do with your time. Enjoy the beauty of My Creation and help Me preserve it." Adam didn't complain. He didn't ask for a negotiation table, for greater benefits, for higher pay. Apparently he accepted the responsibility joyfully as a meaningful assignment from God.

Labor was not a punishment; neither was it an afterthought. *Labor was the design.* It was God's way of filling man's days with pleasant, meaningful activity. Unfortunately, after man's fall into rebellion and sin, the nature of labor was somewhat altered. No longer did the ground yield its fruit willingly; instead, it produced with reluctance, thorns and thistles complicating the task. Sweat and toil and struggle and frustration claimed their place in the picture as the need for labor increased. In spite of this twisting by sin, however, the basic value of human labor remains unchanged. Labor still richly rewards those who accept its yoke and still retains those elements which mark it as God's design for us. Associated with it are invaluable benefits which God willingly directs into our lives as a reward for diligent work.

The Dignity of Work

Have you ever watched a skilled worker in the midst of his labors and noticed the gleam that sparkled in his eyes as he watched the fruit of his efforts slowly ripen and then mature? Have you ever experienced the self-respect, the self-confidence, and the healthy independence that comes when you tackle a difficult task for which you have carefully and patiently prepared? If you have, then you've seen and experienced the dignity of diligent labor.

Not long ago my wife and I hired a professional decorator to hang wallpaper in our house. Always before we had hung wallpaper ourselves, but our last project had taught us a vital lesson. If we wanted to do it right *and* if we wanted to preserve our marriage, we had to hire a pro. In our first house we spent the better part of a weekend in a five-foot by five-foot bathroom, trying to get the wallpaper to stay on the walls. We weren't asking for anything fancy. We just wanted it to stick! We fought, we complained, we climbed all over each other trying to cut the paper and spread the paste. Finally we got the paper on the walls and breathed a sigh of relief, until we noticed the paper shrinking and the lumps rising. We had to pull it down and start again. We spent most of the weekend trying to wallpaper that little bathroom, and the rest of it trying to salvage our marriage. Never again would we try that!

What a treat it was to watch a skilled craftsman. He didn't have to read the directions on the back of the rolls. He didn't have to use a tape measure to check every single move he made. He didn't pour water and paste all over the bathroom floor. He didn't pray as he approached the corner of the medicine cabinet (as I had been compelled to do!). He didn't even buy two extra rolls of paper to compensate for mistakes. He worked quickly and confidently and joyfully, and completed what I considered a two-day job in just a few hours.

I was amazed. "How did you do that?" I inquired. "Did God give you a divine endowment? A special gift? What's your secret?" He smiled innocently and explained. "Practice, that's all. Just practice."

What was he saying in that simple response? He was saying that he had labored diligently over the years to perfect his God-given ability. He had made mistakes, of course, but he had recovered from them, and he had learned to think clearly and organize carefully and execute skillfully. Gradually he had developed confidence in his ability to use what God had given him to accomplish his God-given goal. In short, he had experienced dignity. Diligent labor produces dignity in the man or woman who is willing to commit himself or herself to it.

God knew what dignity would do for a man or woman, and in His grace He designed labor, whether it be in the home or in the marketplace, as a means of helping people develop dignity. Naturally, some people, through no fault of their own, are unable to work. For them God undoubtedly provides another means of developing dignity. But to most people meaningful labor is a viable option, and to them I pose this question: Can people who deliberately refuse to labor develop dignity?

To the generation which preceded mine, there is no need to ask this question. Not only was the value of human labor acknowledged, but it was often so heavily emphasized that it produced the destructive imbalance of workaholism. My generation has recognized the danger of this imbalance, but for many the pendulum has swung too far. Today it is not uncommon for an individual to openly attempt to finagle his way through life without working, with little thought given to the responsibilities of the future. Can this person develop dignity? I think not. Dignity does not float down from heaven; it cannot be purchased nor manufactured. It is a reward reserved for those who labor with diligence.

I've heard it said—and probably some of you reading this book would agree—that dignity is available to a higher degree to those in white-collar jobs who can afford the big homes and fancy cars and who gain the recognition of others. But I beg heartily to differ with this assumption. *Dignity is available to every person in every legitimate, worthwhile profession.*

The farmer who plows the straight furrow, the accountant whose books balance, the truckdriver who backs his 40-foot trailer into a narrow loading dock, the teacher who delivers a well-prepared lesson, the carpenter who keeps the building square, the executive who reads the market accurately, the factory worker who labors with speed and accuracy, the secretary who types the pages perfectly, the student who masters a foreign language, the athlete who plays the game aggressively, the mother who tends the children faithfully, the minister who prepares his sermon and preaches it powerfully—all these people can experience dignity as they commit themselves to their labors.

The writer of the Book of Proverbs says, "Do you see a man skilled in his work? He will stand before kings; he will not stand before obscure men" (22:29). Obviously this doesn't mean that every individual who is skilled in his work will be called to the White House. It does mean, however, that there is a sense of royalty, a sense of honor, associated with diligent labor. Meeting the President face-to-face is not the point. Human dignity is the point. And God has made it available to all who will work.

Responsibility

Labor helps us develop not only dignity, but also a sense of responsibility. In Proverbs 26:13-14 we read, "The sluggard says, 'There is a lion in the road! A lion is in the open square!' Like the door turns on its hinges, so does the sluggard on his bed." The sluggard, the loafer, the person unwilling to commit himself to diligent labor says. "There's a lion on the street." *I cannot go there. I might get hurt. I might be uncomfortable. I might not like it.* He uses every excuse he can conceive to stay away from his labors, and gradually develops a lazy, irresponsible attitude. "As the door turns on its hinges, so does the sluggard on his bed." Unwilling to accept his responsibilities, he turns his back on them, and eventually becomes oblivious to them.

Though most of us learn a certain level of responsibility in the nuclear family and also in school, nowhere do we learn it to the degree that we learn it in the marketplace. Job descriptions, defined duties, performance expectations, ultimatums—they all exert their positive pressure on us. Either we meet the requirements or we lose the job. In this way, the marketplace forces us to accept the challenge of responsible adulthood.

The marketplace teaches us responsibility in two specific areas. The first area is our personal schedules. My own experience illustrates this. During the summers of my high school years, I never had a set curfew. My father allowed me to stay out as late as I chose, provided I was able to be at work on time the next morning. Now, that idea sounded just great to a 16-year-old kid, but there was more wisdom and guidance provided in that demand than I at first realized. You see, each morning I had to begin loading the trucks at our family-owned produce warehouse at 6 o'clock, and I had to work until 5 P.M. Every day. There were no exceptions. How long do you think it took me to learn that I couldn't do a whole day's work on a half night's sleep? Two days. After two days of near insanity, I made the decision. *I will be in bed early every night.* I didn't care what my friends did or what they thought of me. *I will be in bed early, because I must be at work at 6.*

How thankful I am that I learned that lesson early. Diligent labor has provided me with a clear understanding of the needs of my personal schedule. I know that if I have a message to give that requires an unusual amount of study, or if I have traveling or outside speaking engagements to consider, I must adjust my schedule accordingly. I will need to eliminate something else in order to fulfill the requirements of my job. I must properly care for myself physically and emotionally, so that I can be at work on time and produce an honest day's work.

Those on staff at my church know how I feel about promptness. We begin our day at the office at 9:00, not 9:02, or even 9:01. Am I a tyrant? No. I simply believe that I can serve those under my supervision best by teaching them responsibility with regard to their schedules. I do not believe I am hurting them, but rather helping them to develop a habit and a consciousness that will be of value to them for as long as they live. If I can help them learn responsibility with respect to their work schedules, I can then encourage them to be responsible with their time as it relates to their health, their marriages, their ministries, their personal devotions in the morning, etc. My goal, therefore, is not just to get them to work on time, but to teach them a sound principle for living.

Human labor, then, teaches us responsibility in terms of our schedule. It also teaches responsibility with respect to our performance. The words of the marketplace ring loud and clear, "You do your job well, or we will find someone else who will." It's that simple. Though it sounds cold and ruthless, such expectations can be highly motivational to the men and women who willingly accept the challenges of their jobs. In life there are certain things we love to do, and other things we hate to do. So it is in the marketplace. In every job assignment there are certain tasks we pursue with pleasure, and others we abhor. The marketplace says, "You will do them both, or you will do nothing." That, I contend, can be good. It can provide just the challenge and discipline we need.

Once again consider my high school work experience.* Each summer, in addition to our responsibilities at the produce warehouse, my brother and I also had to spend some time working on a farm owned by the company. In late May we began plowing, disking, and dragging the fields, preparing them for planting. In all serious-

---

*Though I don't want to spend too much time talking about myself, I do believe God allowed me to have these experiences so that I could learn personally the lesson of the secular marketplace and share them with others. Throughout this book, any references to myself and my experiences are used only to aid in clarifying a given point.

ness, this job was sheer delight. We took off our shirts, made ourselves comfortable on the tractor seats, and thoroughly enjoyed the sunshine and fresh air. It was a welcome change from the months of winter and classrooms and books.

Unfortunately, in early August, when it was hot and humid and the pleasure of being out in the sun had begun to fade, we had to face a different job which we both dreaded. We had to spray the onion fields with a certain chemical which caused the pupils of our eyes to dilate. Needless to say, pupil dilation causes tremendous pain when you're outside on a bright, sunny day. If we tried to pinch our eyes shut to avoid exposure to the light, we ran over rows of onions, destroying the crop. If we wore sunglasses, the dust and tears combined to cover the glasses with so much grime that again we couldn't see. There was no alternative but to bear the pain and do the best we could.

To this day I claim that was a beneficial experience for us. The farm, our marketplace, taught us that there were certain things we had to do whether we enjoyed them or not. That is the lesson of the marketplace.

Why, you might ask, is that lesson so valuable? Because in all of life we must learn to take the bad with the good. There are times when my relationship with my wife is the source of untold pleasure, when it provides all I need of support and encouragement and human companionship. At other times it is the source of intense frustration and difficulty, even pain. Here then, I can apply the lesson of the marketplace. We don't quit just because times are tough. We accept the bad with the good.

What we learn in the marketplace also spills over into our spiritual lives. At times, putting together messages for my congregation is pure bliss and excitement. At other times, I page through the Bible and can glean nothing from its pages. The experience is drudgery, dry, empty; but still I must stand before an entire church and give a message. I have no choice but to keep working and working and working, until I can discern God's message for the people. Do these times cause me to question my place in the ministry? Do they make me wonder if I am actually walking with the Lord? No, they just remind me again that I must consciously and consistently persevere through times of difficulty.

Remember the sluggard and learn from his ways. Don't create

excuses to keep yourself from your labors. Allow labor to teach you responsibility.

Accomplishment

In the marketplace we learn dignity, we learn responsibility, and finally, we learn to enjoy a sense of accomplishment. After creating our world, God acknowledged that it was "very good" (Gen. 1:31). He expressed and recorded for all time His satisfaction with the world which He had created. It appears to me that He had the emotional vulnerability to tell everyone who reads His Book that the labor of His hands brought Him tremendous pleasure. It was beautiful. It was the product of His love. *It was good.*

Nothing builds self-esteem and self-confidence like accomplishment. Though I maintain some points of contention with the positive thinkers of our day, in this regard I agree with them fully. Success breeds success. When a labor experience results in accomplishment, it provides motivation for the next assignment. Having toiled and cried and sacrificed to see a task through to completion, the laborer experiences the joy of a job well done, and that moves him to begin the cycle again. His success, his sense of accomplishment, prods him back to his labors.

Many claim that because sin has infiltrated this world, feelings of satisfaction and fulfillment are rare and hard to attain. The marketplace, however, affords us regular opportunities to launch and labor over and complete various tasks. As each of these tasks is completed, there is that brief but blessed moment that brings the payoff. Think of the salesman who finally signs the dotted line for the big sale, the student who types the last page of the term paper, the mother who tucks the last child in bed, the doctor who finds the cure, the farmer who finishes the field, the musician who completes the encore, the maintenance worker who turns off the vacuum, the teacher who says, "Class dismissed!" the mason who lays the last brick. To these people, labor graciously affords many moments of accomplishment that can be savored for a lifetime.

In closing this chapter, I quote the great Apostle Paul, who labored joyfully in his ministry and in the secular marketplace as well. "I have fought the good fight, I have finished the course, I have kept the faith; in the future there is laid up for me the crown of righteousness, which the Lord, the righteous Judge, will award to me on that day; and not only to me, but also to all who have loved His appearing" (2 Tim. 4:7-8). Who can love the appearing of the Lord but those who have labored well for Him? Whether in the marketplace or in the ministry, we can labor diligently as unto the Lord, and receive the crown of righteousness, His seal of approval.

Turning again to Scripture, we read the ultimate words of accomplishment, which Jesus uttered from the cross. "It is finished!" (John 19:30) Hanging naked, in agony suspended between heaven and earth, the holy Son of God performed the supreme labor of love. His work in paying for our sins, in securing our eternal redemption, and in opening for us the very doors of life itself, was completed. Surely no greater pain could have been experienced by man, and yet surely no greater joy. His job was finished. Forever. For you and me.

MINISTRY

MARKETPLACE

Two

Christ on the Jobsite

"You are the light of the world. A city set on a hill cannot be hidden. Nor do men light a lamp and put it under the peck-measure, but on the lampstand; and it gives light to all who are in the house. Let your light shine before men in such a way that they may see your good works and glorify your Father who is in heaven" (Matt. 5:14-16).

Imagine Jesus standing on a quiet hillside by the Sea of Galilee speaking quietly to a small band of earnest followers. Then picture, if you will, the marketplace of today. Can you conceive of two more disparate scenes? Yet even today, in the marketplace of a noisy and hectic world, these words find their mark. I am constantly amazed that words which gripped the hearts of first-century believers can still strike responsive chords in the hearts of men and women today. Let me highlight just three ideas illustrated in this passage that have direct bearing on our experiences in the marketplace.

First, Jesus made it absolutely clear that He wants all true believers to radiate His love to those around them. That's why He talked about light. A tiny tungsten filament charged with electrical energy naturally radiates light and dispels darkness. It has no choice. We can't turn a light on and then tell it not to dispel darkness. The very nature of light is such that it *must* shatter the darkness around it. In the same way, true Christians should, by their very nature, radiate something of the work of God in their lives to the people around them. We *are* the light of the world; we must, therefore, radiate that light and dispel darkness.

18

Second, Jesus anticipated that some true believers might choose to limit their candlepower, to refuse to shine their lights. He knew that they would feel safer securely hidden "under the peck-measure" (or in a stained glass sanctuary, perhaps?), where they could bask in their anonymity and escape the accountability associated with "going public" with their faith. He anticipated this and forbade it. "Let your light shine!" He commanded. He did not, and He does not now leave true believers the option of letting their worlds remain in undisturbed blackness.

Finally, Jesus made it obvious that He wants us to spread His influence to *every corner* of this dark, fallen world. It's not enough that we simply take our lights out of hiding. He wants us to put them on the lampstand where everyone can see them! God wants the light of His love to be held high so it can permeate every bit of darkness.

How long will it take for us to realize that *we* are His agents of light? It is through the channels of our daily lives that God shines the light of His message of love.

If fear or embarrassment keep us from being visible channels of God's message, perhaps we need to read Paul's words in Romans 1:16. "For I am not ashamed of the Gospel, for it is the power of God for salvation to everyone who believes, to the Jew first and also to the Greek."

"Why should I be ashamed of the Gospel?" asks Paul. "It is the message of salvation, of life! It's powerful! It is the answer to man's greatest need!"

I try diligently to resist the temptation to prepare and present messages that seek to "excite" or "hype" people into sharing their faith with others. The motivation to be a light to the world should come from the depths of a believer's heart as a result of the genuine work of the Holy Spirit. He might feel inadequate and frightened, and his efforts be feeble and ineffectual, but if he's a true follower of Jesus Christ he should experience a sincere desire to radiate God's message of truth and love to those around him including the people he rubs shoulders with day after day in the marketplace. The million dollar question for most people is "How? How can I most effectively share Christ on the jobsite?"

Well-meaning Christians are often terribly offensive in their attempts to share their faith. Think of the office manager who puts

"Jesus Saves" stickers on everyone's desk. Or imagine the secretary who wears a gold cross around her neck, a "Try God" pin on her collar, and a "Jesus First" bracelet around her wrist. She rattles around the office until her disgusted boss finally screams, "Why are you wearing all that junk?"

"I thought you'd never ask," she replies, and proceeds with her memorized lecture.

Other people use the Bible-verse-on-the-bathroom-walls trick, or they sneak Christian tapes onto the Muzak system. They tack a cheerful "Praise the Lord" onto the end of every conversation, and call their fellow workers "Brother" and "Sister." Oh, they get a response all right—a negative one!

This chapter is a "how to" chapter for spreading the Good News of Christ in the marketplace. What will really make a difference? How can we bring glory to God and touch the lives of the people we meet in a positive, life-changing way?

I believe that our effectiveness for Christ in the marketplace centers on three issues: how we work, who we are, and what we say.

How We Work

In Matthew 5 Jesus did *not* say, "Let your light shine before men in such a way that you can get a promotion and everyone will think you're a great guy." He said, "Let your light shine before men in such a way that they may see your good works *and glorify your Father who is in heaven*" (italics added). What does that mean? It means that if we commit ourselves to diligent and godly labor, the "good works" of the marketplace, we will cause others to marvel at the difference that Christ makes in our lives.

I spent enough years in the marketplace before entering the ministry to know that people in the marketplace always say, "Show me" before they say, "Tell me." Show me the reality of what you believe by the way you live. Then, and only then, will I listen when you tell me about your belief. Another way to say this is that the people who have the greatest positive impact in the marketplace are those who have established the greatest level of credibility in the marketplace. Most people listen only to those whom they have learned to respect.

In light of this, it behooves every Christian to honestly evaluate the level of his or her credibility on the jobsite. In a current television commercial a crusty old gentleman eating a boiled egg claims that his company makes money the old-fashioned way. "We earn it," he says. My friend, the same is true of Christian credibility. It must be earned day by day in the context of the joys and disappointments, the rewards and demands, the successes and failures of the marketplace. There is no shortcut to credibility.

We have to earn it. But how? What are the various threads that must be woven together to create the fabric of credibility? In the next few pages I want to discuss four elements that I believe are basic and necessary to the establishment of a God-honoring level of credibility: a proper attitude toward authority, a willingness to show initiative, a commitment to excellence, and a good, old-fashioned honesty.

Picture in your mind a typical corporate office. In every department four or five people answer to one immediate authority figure, the department head. On the surface all looks calm and peaceful in each department, but behind the scenes a vicious battle rages. In frequent meetings throughout the office, small groups of workers secretly and verbally "beat" their "tyrannical and unreasonable" supervisors. In each of these secret sessions, the conversation reflects the contempt and hostility which often characterizes the attitude of labor toward management in this country today. In the view of the workers, the man in authority is wearing a big black hat. He's the one who judges their work, establishes their deadlines, questions their personal habits and job commitment—and they don't like that. So they complain behind his back and slander his name, all the while giving him marginal cooperation and insincere lip service.

The Bible has something very interesting, even revolutionary, to say about labor/management relations. "Slaves, in all things obey those who are your masters on earth, not with external service, as those who merely please men, but with sincerity of heart, fearing the Lord. Whatever you do, do your work heartily, as for the Lord rather than for men; knowing that from the Lord you will receive the reward of the inheritance. It is the Lord Christ whom you serve" (Col. 3:22-24). Paul speaks openly to the first-century Christians about the proper attitude of slaves toward their earthly masters. Though twentieth-century employees in a free enterprise system are not accustomed to viewing themselves as slaves or their employers as masters, the principles presented in this passage can easily be applied to the contemporary American worksite.

Imagine this group of slaves, young Christians in the church at Colossae, who receive a personal letter from the famed Apostle Paul. As they huddle together to share his written words, their eyes repeatedly gravitate toward the words in Colossians 3:11, "There is no distinction between Greek and Jew, circumcised and uncircumcised, barbarian, Scythian, slave and freeman, but Christ is all, and in all." Imagine their excitement as they read these words. There is no longer to be a distinction between slave and free!

Surely Paul was calling them to break the bonds of human slavery, to face their masters with bold confidence and cry, "We owe you nothing! We're free!" But Paul's intention was not to launch a direct assault on the institution of slavery, however evil it might be. His intention was to transform the master-slave relationship from the inside, by transforming human attitudes.

In verse 11 Paul speaks to these believers of spiritual equality, of the unity of Spirit that joins men and women of different races, different backgrounds, and different social standing into a bond of Christian love. All believers are brothers and sisters, all are children of God, all are forgiven, and all shall receive the inheritance that awaits true followers of Christ.

In verse 22, however, Paul brings these believing slaves back to the practical reality of living godly lives in a world in which they are slaves. Their Christian faith does nothing to change that concrete fact of reality; on a human level, they are still enslaved to earthly masters. Their faith does, however, demand a change in *attitude* toward these earthly masters. "Obey your masters with sincerity of heart," Paul says. No longer is it enough for them to grudgingly fulfill the minimum requirements of their servitude. They are now called to serve from their hearts, willingly!

Undoubtedly, many of them protested against Paul's admonition. "You don't know my master. He sold my children. He raped my wife. If I don't perform to his satisfaction, he whips me. He doesn't deserve Christian respect!"

Do you find yourself wanting to echo those words? Can you hear yourself saying, "That's right, Paul. You don't know my employer. You don't know his habits, his moral life, his moods. It's easy for you to talk about submission, and working diligently, and respecting authority. You never had a boss like mine!"

How we wish that these words written to first-century slaves were not also applicable to twentieth-century employees. But our attempts to avoid the intent of these verses are futile. Their meaning is straightforward and inescapable. It has always fascinated me that, as hard as I may try to explain away a certain passage of Scripture, I just can't do it. I can't change the print! In the end, the literal content of the Word of God stings me with truth.

In verse 22 Paul gives a clear-cut mandate for properly serving our employers. "In all things obey those who are your masters on earth, not with external service, as those who merely please men, but with sincerity of heart, fearing the Lord." "Do your best to please your leaders," he says. "Approach them with a servant's attitude and a genuine willingness to cooperate with them. Don't just give them insincere lip service, grudgingly acquiescing to their demands when they're present, and then showing your true colors when they leave. Serve them sincerely, as if you were serving the Lord."

What would happen in the coffee room at your office if, rather than joining in the hostile attack on your boss, you made a whole-hearted attempt to protect his reputation? I'm not suggesting that you carry his picture in your wallet. I'm not even saying that you have to particularly like him. I am saying, however, that you must openly display an attitude of cooperation and respect and honor because of the biblical imperatives. Did you catch that? *Because of the biblical imperatives.* "Servants, be submissive to your masters with all respect, not only to those who are good and gentle, but also to those who are unreasonable" (1 Peter 2:18). Christians are called to submit to the authority figures in their lives, and not just to those who are kind and good and gentle. Christians are called to go beyond that. We are called to honor even the unreasonable.

But why? Why should we honor even the "dishonorable"? It all goes back to Colossians 3:23-24. "Whatever you do, do your work heartily, as for the Lord rather than for men; knowing that from the Lord you will receive the reward of the inheritance. It is the Lord Christ whom you serve." Ultimately, it is not another man or woman whom we are serving but rather the Lord. And as we serve Him with joy and gladness, we will not only bring honor and glory to His name, but we will also have a positive impact on our co-workers and employers.

If you think that Paul had a one-sided view of authority, be assured that he did not. In Colossians 4:1 he said, "Masters, grant to your slaves justice and fairness, knowing that you too have a Master in heaven." The Christian employ*ee* has a responsibility to approach his employer with respect and an attitude of cooperation; likewise, the Christian employ*er* has a responsibility to treat his employees with fairness and justice. Paul reminds employers that they too are servants, in direct submission to their Master in heaven. As they would hope to have Him treat them, so they should treat their employees.

Needed: A Positive Attitude

If you want to have a positive Christian impact in the marketplace, begin with a positive attitude toward leadership, and then add a willingness to show initiative. "Go to the ant, O sluggard, observe her ways and be wise, which, having no chief, officer or ruler, prepares her food in the summer, and gathers her provision in the harvest" (Pro. 6:6-8). The ant doesn't need someone looking over her shoulder, constantly prodding her to complete her tasks. She knows how to take the initiative. She knows what has to be done and she does it. In the same way, we in the marketplace should pursue our tasks faithfully and diligently, without the need to have someone constantly checking to see that we start on time and do our jobs properly. We may indeed have someone checking us in that way, but it should be because that is the requirement of his job, not because our work demands it. If we complete a given job and no one is available to give us additional direction, we should make every possible effort to creatively fill our free time with work that would benefit our employer.

Christians—and anyone else who wants to build job credibility —must learn to take the initiative. People who do their work without the need for constant pep talks, who are willing to go the extra mile, and who actively look for better, faster, more efficient ways to get the job done are in high demand. They make their work fun. They dive into it enthusiastically and inspire enthusiasm in other people. They create and generate excitement.

After initiative, we must add to our work-style a commitment to excellence. Again, remember Colossians 3:23-24. Whatever you do, pour your heart into it and do it to the best of your ability, as though Christ were the foreman, the inspector, and the owner. Do your work with dedication. Don't do just enough to get by, to meet the lowest standard. For some this may be enough, but not for those of us who desire to establish credibility in the marketplace. We must work in such a way that our service, our product, or our task, even if it is just a tiny step in the overall production process, meets the highest possible standards. Only then will we work in a way pleasing to the Lord.

And don't think that your efforts will go unnoticed. Christ will not forget your dedication to excellence. Verse 24 says that He'll reward our faithful obedience from the spiritual bounty of our eternal inheritance as children of God. Our employer may or may not notice and reward our faithful service, but God will indeed.

Job credibility demands a positive attitude toward authority, a show of initiative, a commitment to excellence, and finally, honesty. One of my neighbors owns a small grocery story and deli in our community, where I stop each morning for my daily cup of coffee. One morning the store owner told me that during the first quarter of that year, he had lost $2,500 worth of inventory, and the loss had been attributed directly to employee theft. "I can't believe it," he said. "I hire good kids who look me straight in the eye and say that they are honest. How can they do this?"

The statistics are staggering. Many store owners fear their employees more than they fear shoplifters. What benefit is there in attempting to curb shoplifting if their own employees undermine the effort? It's a most discouraging situation.

What does the Bible say about this? "Let him who steals steal no longer" (Eph. 4:28). Do we need a more direct statement on the subject? Need we doubt God's mind in this matter? Don't steal. It's that simple. And this doesn't apply only to merchandise. Don't steal from the time clock. Don't take unscheduled breaks. Don't expand lunch hours. Obey company rules regarding personal phone calls. Don't misuse expense money. There are a thousand ways to steal, and God forbids every one of them.

A friend of mine has been praying for and gently witnessing to his employer for years. Not long ago his employer was visited by a former employee who said, "You may not even remember me, but I worked for you many years ago. One day I stole a case of oil from you. I knew you'd never miss it, so I didn't give it much thought.

Since that time, however, I have become a Christian, and I know that before God I must make it right with you, so here's my check for the oil. I apologize to you and assure you that such behavior is no longer a part of my lifestyle." That encounter had more impact on that nonbelieving employer than a Bible study or a church service or a memorized verse could ever have had. He was genuinely moved by the practical effect that Christ had on the man's life.

I can't leave this subject without making a simple, direct statement. If you're a believer and you are guilty of taking anything—pencils, paperclips, money, clothes, food, etc.—from your company, please make a commitment right now to confess to your employer and make it right. When Zaccheus, the famous tax collector, became a Christian, he went straight to the people he had wronged and made restitution to them. In fact, he was so eager to make right his sin and honor the Lord that he said, "Behold, Lord, half of my possessions I will give to the poor, and if I have defrauded anyone of anything, I will give back four times as much" (Luke 19:8).

If you have been dishonest in any way, make restitution. Your honesty will make a powerful statement to your employer about the work of God in your life.

Who You Are

If we manifest proper attitudes toward leadership, display godly initiative, and commit ourselves to excellence and honesty, our work will earn for us the level of credibility we need to bring a Christian influence into the marketplace. But how we work is only the beginning, and must be supported by who we are. Some may ask why I place *who we are* second to *how we work*. Should not what we *do* be secondary to what we *are*? Ideally it should be, of course, but in the marketplace where the bottom line is output, productivity, and service, how we work is the first thing that people will notice about us. Still, for the Christian it is only the beginning. We must support our godly work pattern with a godly way of life.

One summer while I was in college, my father hired a West Point graduate to work at the produce company. The truckdrivers and the other dock help were thrilled! They were rough, uneducated, hard-drinking, hard-fighting, women-chasing men who relished the opportunity to make sport of a nice, clean-cut, all-American West Point grad. It was going to be a great summer for them. Then a rumor broke. The kid was not only a wet-behind-the-ears college boy—he was a Christian too! That was all the men needed to hear. They were more determined than ever to make the summer miserable for him.

But they didn't. In one short summer David, the all-American boy, turned our company upside down. It all started on his first day at work, when he walked behind the warehouse to eat his lunch. He sat down on an old pile of wood, took out his lunch box and his Bible, and started teaching a Bible study to a small group of vagrants who lived in an old railroad boxcar. As if that wasn't enough, he shared his lunch with them.

Boy, did the other men laugh at him! I even laughed a little myself. Those old beggars had been around for years. We knew them well. What a waste of time. What could David hope to accomplish with them?

But before long we noticed that a beautiful transformation had taken place. The old boxcar was no longer the private haven of two or three beggars who waited to share David's meager lunch; it had become a sanctuary for battered, beaten men who came to hear the Word of God. David's one-man lunch couldn't fill their emptiness. It was the Word of God they sought—and they really listened. They were being touched in a visible, life-changing way.

Gradually some of the other employees, hardened men who had vowed to cut this West Point kid down to size, began to enjoy having David around. They started talking to him during their coffee breaks. They began asking him for advice, even asking him to pray for their kids. We should have paid David to be the company counselor! He could have placed a sign over the refrigerator room door and started a professional counseling service.

During the course of one summer, David had an impact on all of us because he lived a loving, Christlike life in the marketplace. He treated people the way Christ treated people. He was kind and gentle. His words were filled with affirmation and encouragement. He was cheerful. He displayed quiet dignity, deep-seated security, and strength of character that drew people to him like a magnet. He worked hard, but he never seemed to lose sight of people.

The shame of the marketplace is that so often it centers on nothing but business. Workers strive to finish their projects and reach their goals without giving a thought to anything else. They become frightfully robotlike, going through the motions of relating to people without emotion, and developing friendships devoid of feeling and empathy.

People Were Jesus' Business

Even Jesus' disciples became so caught up in their responsibilities that they sometimes forgot about people. When mothers tried to bring their children to Jesus so He could touch them, the disciples rebuked them. They didn't want those noisy little kids getting in the way and hindering the work of the Lord. Matthew records Jesus' response to this attitude, "Let the children alone, and do not hinder them from coming to Me; for the kingdom of heaven belongs to such as these" (Matt. 19:14). They were more important than His schedule and His output quota for the day.

What about us? Are not people our business too? Sure we have to watch the schedule and the output quotas, but that's only part of our calling. Our higher calling is to people. Yes, to people. The Apostle Paul challenges us to "walk in a manner worthy of the calling with which [we] have been called, with all humility and gentleness, with patience, showing forbearance to one another in love" (Ephesians 4:1-2). When we start treating people on the job the way Christ treated them, and the way Paul calls us to treat one another, we will begin to have a Christian influence in the marketplace.

Who we are in our relationships, our language, our jokes, our dispositions, our reactions to disappointment, in all situations that make up our workday, will combine with how we work to establish our credibility in such a way that people will listen to what we say.

What We Say

If we are genuine believers who work diligently and behave in a loving, Christlike manner, what we say will have a positive impact on those who hear. Most people would like to believe that if they act like Christians and work hard, people around them will automatically respond to their "living example" and become Christians. But that's absurd. The Word of God must be articulated by believers before it can evoke a response in nonbelievers. That is to say, the presentation of the Gospel message must include an intelligent explanation that can lead to cognitive understanding, and we've been given the task of presenting that explanation.

The Apostle Peter urges, "But sanctify Christ as Lord in your hearts, always being ready to make a defense to everyone who asks you to give an account for the hope that is in you, yet with gentleness and reverence" (1 Peter 3:15). This doesn't mean we have to hit people over the head with the Gospel. It does mean, however, that we should always be prepared to respond gently, with clarity and accuracy, when someone asks us about our faith or when the Holy Spirit opens our eyes to a person's need for the Lord and prompts us to share God's message with him.

I have been given the responsibility to work hard, walk with Christ, and speak the Gospel message clearly in my marketplace. You've been given the same responsibility in your marketplace. Let us yield ourselves to God's direction in this matter, by being prepared to share our faith in a personal, loving, understandable way. Let us take our God-given responsibility seriously.

Honored Slave Boy

The story of Joseph, the favorite son of the Jewish patriarch Jacob, illustrates every point of this chapter beautifully. Joseph's envious brothers sold him to a caravan of traders who took Joseph into Egypt and sold him into slavery. Like thousands of Israelites before him, Joseph appeared to be treading a sure path to lifelong servitude and humble oblivion. But at this point, Joseph's story takes an interesting turn.

"Now Joseph had been taken down to Egypt; and Potiphar, an Egyptian officer of Pharaoh, the captain of the bodyguard, bought him from the Ishmaelites, who had taken him down there. And the Lord was with Joseph, so he became a successful man. And he was in the house of his master, the Egyptian. Now his master saw that the Lord was with him and how the Lord caused all that he did to prosper in his hand. So Joseph found favor in his sight, and became his personal servant; and he made him overseer over his house, and all that he owned he put in his charge. And it came about that from the time he made him overseer in his house, and over all that he owned, the Lord blessed the Egyptian's house on account of Joseph; thus the Lord's blessing was upon all that he owned, in the house and in the field. So he left everything he owned in Joseph's charge; and with him around he did not concern himself with anything except the food which he ate" (Gen. 39:1-6).

What an incredible story! From favored son to common slave to trusted overseer, Joseph lived a life that glorified God. *How Joseph worked* gave his master a reason to promote him to a position of highest authority; *who Joseph was* allowed his master to trust him with everything he owned; and *what Joseph said* made it clear to his master that it was God's work in Joseph that brought about his success. Think about this. Potiphar was not a God-fearing man himself, but he so clearly saw God at work in Joseph that he was free to have complete confidence in Joseph, and to give honor to Joseph's God.

Up to this point, Joseph lived the perfect rags to riches story. But in verses 7-10 we see trouble. "And it came about after these events that his master's wife looked with desire at Joseph, and she said, 'Lie with me.' But he refused and said to his master's wife, 'Behold, with me here, my master does not concern himself with anything in the house, and he has put all that he owns in my charge. There is no one greater in this house than I, and he has withheld nothing from me except you, because you are his wife. How then could I do this great evil, and sin against God?' And it came about as she spoke to Joseph day after day, that he did not listen to her to lie beside her, or be with her." If there was ever an opportunity to be dishonest, this was it. Only Potiphar's wife had been withheld from Joseph, and now she too was available to him. What was his response? "How can I do this great evil, and sin against God?" Faced with a potentially overwhelming temptation, Joseph chose to turn away from it and bring honor to God's name.

Unfortunately, Potiphar's wife didn't appreciate Joseph's rejection, so she framed him, claimed that he had violated her, resulting in Potiphar's putting him in jail.

"But the Lord was with Joseph and extended kindness to him, and gave him favor in the sight of the chief jailer. And the chief jailer committed to Joseph's charge all the prisoners who were in the jail; so that whatever was done there, he was responsible for it. The chief jailer did not supervise anything under Joseph's charge because the Lord was with him; and whatever he did, the Lord made to prosper" (Gen. 39:21-23). Even in jail, Joseph's credibility was irresistible. From common criminal Joseph rose to head jailer, and eventually he was out on the streets again to become the second highest ruler in the land, subject only to Pharaoh himself.

In Genesis 41:39-43 we read, "So Pharaoh said to Joseph, . . . 'There is no one so discerning and wise as you are. You shall be over my house, and according to your command all my people shall do homage; only in the throne I will be greater than you. . . . See I have set you over all the land of Egypt.' Then Pharaoh took off his signet ring from his hand, and put it on Joseph's hand, and clothed him in garments of fine linen, and put the gold necklace around his neck. And he had him ride in his second chariot; and they proclaimed before him, 'Bow the knee!' And he set him over all the land of Egypt."

Joseph fulfilled the requirements of his job in such a way that he was rewarded with responsibility and honor. Does that mean that everyone who establishes such credibility will climb the corporate ladder? Is that the message of this story? Probably not. History seems to have proven that not every godly man or woman who honors the Lord in his or her work will rise to prominence. Even Joseph's life illustrates that godliness is not always rewarded with personal advancement. On the contrary, Joseph ended up in jail because of his commitment to honesty!

We should not focus our attention on Joseph's rise to fame and fortune, but on his humble obedience to God which allowed him to leave a godly mark on his world. Whether he was in jail or in a position of national honor, he worked, lived and spoke in such a way that he earned the trust and confidence of other people and he directed their attention toward God.

Let us learn from his example!

Three

Modern-Day Prophets

As Jesus traveled through the cities and villages of Israel, proclaiming the Gospel and healing the sick, He was moved with compassion for the multitudes who followed Him. They were distressed and downcast, like sheep without a shepherd. They needed His message, His love, and His forgiveness, so they could experience life abundant and eternal. "The harvest is plentiful," He said, "but the workers are few. Therefore, beseech the Lord of the harvest to send out workers into His harvest" (Matt. 9:37-38). The needy lost were there, and the message was waiting to be given, but where were the laborers, the spokespersons for God's Word?

I am always disappointed to hear sincere Christians say that if they had their lives to live over again, they would be foreign missionaries so that they could really serve the Lord! The Bible teaches repeatedly that we are *all* missionaries, no matter where we are. We are missionaries to our families, to our neighbors, and to the world of people we rub shoulders with in the marketplace. By how we work, who we are, and what we say, we can bring a Christian influence to our jobsite that can have far-reaching effects in the lives of men and women who desperately need to hear of God's forgiveness, and we can bring honor and glory to the name of our Lord.

I assumed in chapter 2 and in the introduction to this chapter that Christians actually believe that if God has called them to work in the marketplace, He has also called them to be missionaries in the marketplace. Without that assumption, there is no reason to talk about bringing "the light of Christ" to the marketplace; there is no need to concern ourselves with Christian credibility; and there is surely no need to learn to articulate our faith.

But have I made that assumption carelessly? Do you really believe that you have been called to be Christ's light to your marketplace?

I fear that many Christians believe deep down inside that taking the Gospel to the marketplace is someone else's responsibility, or at least they hope it is. They long for a way to cast the responsibility on someone else's shoulders without guilt or shame.

The Old Testament records the story of a prophet of God who felt the same way. He felt that God's call to him was unjust. He did not want to accept the responsibility of taking God's words to a pagan world. He did not want to deal with the inconvenience and the risk of being God's messenger. In short, his life parallels the lives of many contemporary Christians.

Take Jonah, for Example

"The word of the Lord came to Jonah the son of Amittai saying, 'Arise, go to Nineveh the great city, and cry against it, for their wickedness has come up before Me'" (Jonah 1:1). Jonah was a Hebrew prophet living in Israel when God called him to go to the city of Nineveh, in the country of Assyria. I don't know whether God appeared to Jonah in a vision, or spoke to him in an audible voice, or simply gave His call through the inner witness of the Holy Spirit in Jonah's life, but whatever His means of revelation, He made it clear that Jonah was handpicked to take His message of judgment to the people Nineveh.

Verse 3 reveals Jonah's response to God's call. "But Jonah rose up to flee to Tarshish from the presence of the Lord. So he went down to Joppa, found a ship which was going to Tarshish, paid the fare, and went down into it to go with them to Tarshish from the presence of the Lord." Jonah was not interested in God's call. Instead of heading east and making the three-day walk to Nineveh, he bought passage on a ship traveling west to Tarshish.

When the Prophet Samuel received his call from the Lord, he said, "Speak, for Thy servant is listening" (I Sam. 3:10). When Isaiah received his call, he said, "Here am I. Send me!" (Isa. 6:8)

But, when Jonah received his call to Nineveh, he said, "Stop, Lord! I don't want to hear another word. Send someone else. I don't want the call!"

What was wrong with Jonah? The Almighty God of the universe made a claim on his life and called him into action, and Jonah said no! What was his problem? Why did he reject the call?

I think the answer is simple. Jonah had no love for the lost. He had no concern in his heart for those who were living without the knowledge of God's forgiveness. He was a Hebrew, a child of God's chosen people. Why should he care about pagan nonbelievers? What was Nineveh to him? The other prophets were called to bring cleansing and healing to Israel. Why did God choose him to go into enemy territory, into the land of the evil Assyrians? His family was safe, chosen, godly, and well taken care of. Why did he have to worry about the rest of the world? As far as he was concerned, *it wasn't his problem!*

Besides, he would look like a fool, preaching a message of judgment to the men of Nineveh. Imagine walking through the streets of Nineveh crying, "Yet 40 days and Nineveh will be overthrown" (Jonah 3:4). The people would mock him, laugh at him, and cast him out of the city. No, he wasn't going to subject himself to that. So, he traveled to the Mediterranean Sea, paid his fare, went into the hold of the ship, and fell asleep. Perhaps if he slept he wouldn't have to deal with the consequences of his disobedience.

"Why Are You Sleeping, Jonah?"

But sleep could not shelter Jonah from God's anger. "And the Lord hurled a great wind on the sea and there was a great storm on the sea so that the ship was about to break up. Then the sailors became afraid, and every man cried to his god, and they threw the cargo which was in the ship into the sea to lighten it for them. But Jonah had gone below into the hold of the ship, lain down, and fallen sound asleep. So the captain approached him and said, 'How is it that you are sleeping? Get up, call on your god. Perhaps your god will be concerned about us so that we will not perish.' And each man said to his mate, 'Come, let us cast lots so we may learn on whose account this calamity has struck us.' So they cast lots and the lot fell on Jonah" (Jonah 1:4-8).

"Do not be deceived, God is not mocked; for whatever a man

sows, this he will also reap" (Gal. 6:7). Jonah could not spurn God's call without invoking God's wrath. Nor could he ignore the consequences of his disobedience. He had only one alternative: confession to God and to the men with him on the ship. So he said to them, "'I am a Hebrew, and I fear the Lord God of heaven who made the sea and the dry land.' Then the men became extremely frightened and they said to him, 'How could you do this?' For the men knew that he was fleeing from the presence of the Lord, because he had told them. So they said to him, 'What should we do to you that the sea may become calm for us?'—for the sea was becoming increasingly stormy. And he said to them, 'Pick me up and throw me into the sea. Then the sea will become calm for you, for I know that on account of me this great storm has come upon you'" (Jonah 1:9-12).

Unwilling to cast Jonah to certain death, the seamen attempted to row to land, but their efforts were in vain. Ultimately, they were forced to throw Jonah into the raging sea, and immediately the waters became calm. "Then the men feared the Lord greatly, and they offered a sacrifice to the Lord and made vows. And the Lord appointed a great fish to swallow Jonah, and Jonah was in the stomach of the fish three days and three nights" (Jonah 1:16-17).

One short chapter of Scripture tells of Jonah's call from God, of Jonah's blatant rejection of that call, of the consequences of Jonah's disobedience, and of Jonah's thorough confession. Then God called a second time to Jonah. After commanding the great fish to vomit Jonah out onto dry land, God said, "Arise, go to Nineveh the great city and proclaim to it the proclamation which I am going to tell you" (Jonah 3:2).

Needless to say, Jonah obeyed. He walked around the mighty city of the brave Assyrian warriors and proclaimed God's judgment on them and warned them that they would be overthrown in 40 days.

I doubt if Jonah's heart was really in his preaching. He probably still felt self-conscious and foolish. But what a response his message received! "Then the people of Nineveh believed in God; and they called a fast and put on sackcloth from the greatest to the least of them. When the word reached the king of Nineveh, he arose from his throne, laid aside his robe from him, covered himself with sackcloth, and sat on the ashes. And he issued a proclamation and it said, 'In Nineveh by the decree of the king and his nobles: Do not let man, beast, herd, or flock taste a thing. Do not let them eat or drink water. But both man and beast must be covered with sackcloth; and let men call on God earnestly that each may turn from his wicked way and from the violence which is in his hands. Who knows, God may turn and relent, and withdraw His burning anger so that we shall not perish?'" (Jonah 3:5-9)

From the king to the poorest beggar, the people of Nineveh repented of their wickedness, clothed themselves in the humility of sackcloth and ashes, and cast themselves on God's mercy. God accepted their repentance, forgave them, and withdrew His threat of destruction.

Comparison in Compassion

One would expect Jonah to be thrilled at the Ninevites' response to his preaching, thrilled that an entire city had been spared God's judgment. "But it greatly displeased Jonah, and he became angry" (Jonah 4:1). Jonah was angry because God had withdrawn His promised judgment from the Ninevites, leaving Jonah standing in embarrassment with an unfulfilled message of doom. Jonah was disappointed that God *didn't* destroy the city!

"Therefore now, O Lord," says Jonah in verse 3, "please take my life from me, for death is better to me than life." In overwhelming self-pity, Jonah begs for God to release him from the anguish of life.

It is at this point that God exposes the root of Jonah's disobedience, his anger, and his self-pity. God didn't use a theology book to show Jonah the error of his ways, nor even well-chosen words; He simply grew a little plant.

"Then Jonah went out from the city and sat east of it. There he made a shelter for himself and sat under it in the shade until he could see what would happen in the city. So the Lord God appointed a plant and it grew up over Jonah to be a shade over his head to deliver him from his discomfort. And Jonah was extremely happy about the plant" (Jonah 4:5-6).

I can almost hear Jonah's words. "This is the first good thing that has happened to me in weeks! I was tossed into the raging Mediterranean Sea, gulped into the stomach of a great fish, and vomited up onto the seashore. Then I had to parade around like a fool proclaiming a false judgment on Nineveh. It's about time something good happened to me! It was long overdue!"

Little did Jonah know that God was not yet finished with him or his precious little plant. "But God appointed a worm when dawn came the next day, and it attacked the plant and it withered. And it came about when the sun came up that God appointed a scorching east wind, and the sun beat down on Jonah's head so that he became faint and begged with all his soul to die, saying, 'Death is better to me than life'" (Jonah 4:7-8). It wasn't enough that God had brought misfortune and humiliation into Jonah's life; now He was taking from Jonah the one thing that had brought him comfort, his plant. Again Jonah asked for death.

In the next three verses the purpose of this whole beautiful object lesson becomes obvious. "Then God said to Jonah, 'Do you have good reason to be angry about the plant?' And he said, 'I have good reason to be angry, even to death.' Then the Lord said, 'You had compassion on the plant for which you did not work, and which you did not cause to grow, which came up overnight and perished overnight. And, should I not have compassion on Nineveh, the great city in which there are more than 120,000 persons who do not know the difference between their right and left hand, as well as many animals?'" (Jonah 4:9-11)

It's as if God were saying, "Jonah, you got all emotional and upset about that little plant, and you had *nothing* to do with its creation or its growth! It sprang up in one day and then it was gone, yet you developed such an attachment to it that you grieve its loss. Can't you see how much more I am attached to the people of Nineveh, whom I created? Jonah, I breathed life into them! I helped them grow and mature into the men and women they are today. Oh, yes, I know they were wicked, but that's because they were ignorant. They did not know their right hand from their left with respect to spiritual truth. They just needed a prophet, Jonah—you! And now they have responded to your words. That's what excites *Me! People!* People who repent of their rebellion and seek Me with sincere hearts. You cared about a green plant that lasted for one day. Don't you care about *people?*"

Application

What pains God took to impress on Jonah his need to respond to God's call! Surely He desires that we modern-day prophets would learn that lesson. How will the message of Christ reach the unbelievers in the marketplace, our Nineveh, if we refuse to respond to God's call with loving hearts?

Jesus said to His followers, "You shall be My witnesses" (Acts 1:8) and "You are the light of the world" (Matt. 5:14). The Apostle Peter admonished believers to "sanctify Christ as Lord in your hearts, always being ready to make a defense to everyone who asks you to give an account for the hope that is in you, yet with gentleness and reverence" (1 Peter 3:15). Need we doubt God's call?

"The harvest is plentiful, but the workers are few," Jesus said (Matt. 9:37). Will we be His workers? His prophets? His missionaries to the marketplace?

For centuries, Christians have rejected Christ's call on their lives by claiming that the people "out there," in the world or in the marketplace, are not their responsibility. We quote the preachers who tell us that our responsibility is to our families; only "if we have time" should we move out to the world "beyond."* But, of course, we never have the time.

Besides, like Jonah, we feel a little foolish. We don't want to talk about sin, a crucified Saviour, and salvation. We are too sophisticated for that. It's just not our style.

I confess with shame that there was a time in my ministry when I was anything but bold with the truth. I was more concerned with impressing the public than I was with preaching the truth. And I hate that part of my past.

Thank God that we can confess, just as Jonah did. We can repent of our hardheartedness and our self-centered isolation. We can call our callousness sin and seek God's forgiveness.

Jonah knew how to repent. He said, "Throw me into the sea. I deserve it." Can we join him in such honest confession? We need to say, "Lord, I am disgustingly self-centered. I am obsessed with approval. I don't want to give the message with boldness. Forgive me. Help me. Change me."

After confessing his sin and accepting God's forgiveness, Jonah received his second call. In His grace, God rescued Jonah from the

---

*I too recognize that our *first* responsibility is to our families, but that should never be used as an excuse to avoid our responsibility to the other people whose lives we touch.

churning sea, returned him to dry ground, and once again entrusted him with a message for the Ninevites. We too, like Jonah, can receive God's forgiveness and a second call, a call to enter the marketplace as a modern-day prophet.

We have compared ourselves to Jonah in terms of our call, our frequent rejection of that call, our confession, and our second call. Now, what about our compassion? Do we too love plants more than people? Do our emotions become more kindled by the pleasures of life than by seeing the lost find the Lord? What is it that makes our hearts beat fast with anticipation and excitement? What is it that keeps us rising early in the morning to ask for God's blessing and guidance on our day?

It is God's nature to be incurably and eternally concerned about the plight of people. Those of us who have His Spirit residing in our hearts should also have that same emotional reaction and love for people who are without the Lord.

When we started Willow Creek Community Church, we lacked money, experience, knowledge, and a host of other important tools, but one thing we did not lack was a concern for the lost. We knocked on doors and made phone calls and placed newspaper ads to make contact with people who needed God's message. We couldn't help but hurt for the people who were walking in spiritual darkness.

The people that we rub shoulders with day in and day out need modern-day prophets. Sharing our faith with people may be risky; it may cause us some embarrassment or discomfort. But is that price too much to pay? Will it eternally scar us to be laughed at or humiliated now and then? Should we not be willing to suffer just a little for the sake of Christ and those whom He loves?

How to Be a Modern-Day Prophet

If we choose to be modern-day prophets, where do we begin? What are the necessary tools?

First, we need the willingness of the Old Testament prophet, Isaiah. In Isaiah 6:8 we read, "Then I heard the voice of the Lord, saying, 'Whom shall I send, and who will go for Us?' Then I said, 'Here am I. Send me!'" He heard God's call and responded with a willing heart. He knew God's need for a messenger, and he was eager to fill that need. God did not have to twist his arm (or send him into the belly of a whale).   Isaiah was ready to go.

Next, we need the heart of Jeremiah, who is known as the "weeping prophet" because his love for people so often brought him to tears.   Perhaps we need to pray that God's love will so spill over into our hearts that we will know the meaning of a tear shed for needy men and women.

We also need the boldness of Peter, the New Testament teacher who was threatened with imprisonment if he continued to share his faith in the public arena. Acts 4:19-20 records his response to the authorities who threatened him. "Whether it is right in the sight of God to give heed to you rather than to God, you be the judge; for we cannot stop speaking what we have seen and heard." After saying those words, Peter joined in prayer with the other believers, and then went out "and began to speak the Word of God with boldness" (Acts 4:31).

We need the willingness of Isaiah, the heart of Jeremiah, the boldness of Peter, and now, the perseverance of Paul. Arrested, beaten, stoned, shipwrecked, imprisoned, and falsely accused, Paul was still able to say to the Christian converts at Colossae, "I rejoice in my sufferings for your sake" (Col. 1:24). He was willing to suffer repeated abuse for preaching the message of Christ as long as it meant that someone would come to know Christ.

And this brings us to the last necessary tool. We need the message of Christ. When someone comes to us with a sincere desire to repent of his sins and turn in humility to Christ, he doesn't need *our* opinions or human philosophies. He needs the true message of salvation through Jesus Christ.

I have made it a point to keep in mind a simple means of explaining the Gospel of Jesus. It begins with Romans 3:23, "For all have sinned and fall short of the glory of God." None of us are able to meet God's standard of moral excellence; we are all sinners. The second step is Romans 6:23, "For the wages of sin is death, but the free gift of God is eternal life in Christ Jesus our Lord." The natural result of our sin is eternal death, or separation from God, but because of Christ's substitutionary death on the cross, God can offer us total forgiveness and eternal life. The last step is Romans 10:13, "For whoever will call upon the name of the Lord will be saved."

I know it's a simple outline. All it talks about is sin, the Saviour, and salvation. But that's about all we need to know to begin to be modern-day prophets. That simple message can be used to affect people's lives for eternity.

We all have the tendency to avoid the sin issue. The message would be so much more comfortable without it. But, unless men and women are aware of their sin, they won't recognize their need for a Saviour who offers eternal life to all who call on His name.

Daily we each walk into a world of people who do not know their right hand from their left when it comes to the issues of eternity. They need a modern-day prophet.

Are we willing? Are you willing?

Our bank accounts, our summer homes, our late-model cars will all rust and rot and depreciate, but the people we touch for Christ will live on into eternity.

Four

Handling Anger

In this chapter I want to discuss another subject that has deep implications for the Christian who really wants to glorify God in his workplace. In marriages, families, clubs, schools, social groups, and of course the marketplace, disagreement leads to tension which leads to anger, and in most cases anger leads to broken relationships. Why? Because very few people know how to deal constructively with anger. This, then, is the subject of this chapter: how to successfully handle anger and mend broken relationships.

One of the trademarks of the mature follower of Jesus Christ is the love which permeates his interpersonal relationships (Ps. 133:1; Rom. 15:5). He displays a graciousness, a tenderness, and a sensitivity toward other people, not just in his church, but in his family, in his school, in his neighborhood, and of course in his workplace.

We are told in 2 Corinthians 5:17, "Therefore if any man is in Christ, he is a new creature; the old things passed away; behold, new things have come." What are these "old things" that have passed away? For many of us they are the old feelings of anger, hatred, or malice that formerly characterized our interpersonal relationships. Through the cleaning work of the Holy Spirit, these attitudes have been transformed so that we can look at others through new eyes washed in the love of God. When we become Christians we become new beings, and this "newness" should be reflected in qualities such as humility, gentleness, patience, love, kindness, and forgiveness.

To live in harmony with others is not an option for the Christian; it is a command. Jesus said in John 13:34-35. "A new commandment I give to you, that you love one another, even as I have loved you, that you also love one another. By this all men will know that you are My disciples, if you have love for one another." Our love for one another provides evidence that we are, in fact, true followers of Jesus.

This concept is presented again in 1 John 4:20-21: "If someone says, 'I love God,' and hates his brother, he is a liar; for the one who does not love his brother whom he has seen, cannot love God whom he has not seen. And this commandment we have from Him, that the one who loves God should love his brother also." One way, then, to test the genuineness of our Christian faith is to ask ourselves these questions: Do I make every effort to live in peace with other people? Can I walk in love even when that becomes difficult? Am I earnestly attempting to establish a bond of unity in my marriage? Are my social relationships characterized by harmony? Do I have a growing sensitivity to others? Am I patient, displaying an attitude of forbearance? Do I, in the practical realities of daily life, truly "love my brother"?

The true believer should long for harmony in every relationship he has. When a relationship is broken he should experience a godly sorrow that leads him to repeated, determined efforts toward reconciliation and restoration so that he can honestly say, "To my knowledge, at this moment, God is being glorified in every relationship I have."

Can you say that about every relationship you have? Do your friendships and family relationships give God glory? Does the condition of each of your human relationships make a positive statement about your relationship with God? Do your encounters with other people enhance God's credibility or His honor in this world? Though every area of our lives makes a statement about the reality of our Christian faith, perhaps none of them will have a more powerful effect on the way other people view our God than our interpersonal relationships.

The material in this chapter was originally used in a series of messages on anger. While working on that series, I realized to my discredit that when I allowed anger to disrupt a relationship that was important to me, I immediately became concerned about it and was eager to take steps to bring about reconciliation and restoration. However, when my anger disrupted a relationship that was not particularly important to me, I had a tendency to ignore it. I found myself thinking, "Well, I may never see that person again, anyway. Why bother to restore the relationship? It would be different if we were close friends. But in this case, does it really matter?"

It is with shame that I confess that ungodly attitude. The truth as revealed in Scripture is that the glory of God is at stake in every relationship we have. God wants every relationship we have to be characterized by a peaceful harmony, even if it involves someone we may never see again (Heb. 12:14). He wants every relationship we have to honor Him.

Is that true for you? What about your spouse? Your ex-spouse? Your neighbors? Your teachers? Your in-laws? Your children? Your employer? Your former employer? It's important to take frequent inventory of our relationships and honestly determine whether or not God is being glorified in them.

God places such a high premium on relational harmony that Jesus said, 'But I say to you that everyone who is angry with his brother shall be guilty . . . and whoever shall say, 'You fool,' shall be guilty enough to go into the fiery hell" (Matt. 5:22). Unresolved anger, and the terms of degradation that unmask it, are not taken lightly by God. Poisonous, hateful, spite-filled emotions are foreign to the character of God and should be foreign to the heart that has been melted by the love of Jesus Christ.

But that's the ideal. The reality is that often it takes only a hostile word, an unkind rumor, or a minor disagreement to prompt an outpouring of anger that can totally destroy a relationship. What do we do when that happens? Do we throw up our hands in despair and plead helplessness? Do we resign ourselves to living in a world of broken relationships?

The Bible says that at that point we need to take immediate action to restore the relationship. "Be angry, and yet do not sin; do not let the sun go down on your anger, and do not give the devil an opportunity" (Eph. 4:26-27). Before the evil one has the opportunity to intensify our feelings of anger and square us off in opposing corners, ready for battle, we need to begin the process of reconciliation.

"If therefore you are presenting your offering at the altar, and there remember that your brother has something against you, leave your offering there before the altar, and go your way; first be reconciled to your brother, and then come and present your offering" (Matt. 5:23-24). Though the believer who has been redeemed by Christ no longer needs to lay an earthly sacrifice on the altar (as in the animal sacrifices of Bible times), we are called to lay our lives before the Lord daily as a sacrifice of love and service. If in so doing we remember that we have a broken relationship, we have no recourse but to seek a reconciliation. God cannot fully accept our lives of sacrifice and our offerings of love as long as we harbor the impurity of unresolved anger.

In our efforts toward reconciliation are not accepted by the person with whom we have the problem, we are no longer held responsible for the division. However, it must be emphasized over and over again that God will not be satisfied with halfhearted attempts toward unity. We are to make every possible effort toward establishing harmony. If our efforts are in vain, we should be able to say with complete honesty, "I did everything in my power to establish peace."

The Scripture passages we have looked at in this chapter are of the kind that "separate the men from the boys" in Christian circles. It's one thing to hear the Word of God; but it is another thing entirely to let it so convict us that we submit to it in humble obedience.

What makes reconciliation so difficult is that often we really don't want to reconcile. We enjoy our anger. We want to nurse and nurture it. We believe that it's justified and that we deserve this opportunity to relish it. It takes an unprecedented amount of moral resolve to acknowledge those feelings and submit them to the Lord. It's hard to say, "God, I don't feel like resolving this anger, but I do want to be obedient. Help me be a doer of Your Word, not just a hearer. Give me the courage and strength to attempt, with all sincerity, the reconciliation that will please You."

While I was originally preparing this material for a message, a man with whom I had a broken relationship came to me after a church service and said, "I'd like to meet with you tomorrow and talk about restoring our relationship."

I have to confess to you that at that moment I was unable to muster enough emotional energy to say, "Sure, that's great. Let's do it." My relationship with that man had been on a roller coaster for five years. Over and over again we had seemingly resolved our differences and restored our relationship, only to have it disrupted again by a new wind of dissension. My thoughts at the moment of his request were: *Why bother? We've tried so many times before and it never worked. Besides, he doesn't even live here anymore. At the most we only see one another once a year. Does it really matter?*

I responded halfheartedly. "OK, maybe. I'll check my schedule." As he turned to leave I added, "Call me tomorrow."

I was hoping, of course, that he wouldn't call, but he did. And was I glad! During the 24 hours since our previous conversation, I'd realized that I had to obey the Word of God. I couldn't call myself a Christian without making every possible effort to bring about a reconciliation. I said, "Thanks for calling. My schedule is clear. Let's get together right now!"

In the conversation that we shared that afternoon, we were able to uncover the fundamental problem that had been haunting our relationship for five years. The result was a genuine reconciliation that totally transformed the tense relationship we had endured for so long. What a release of freedom and joy we experienced that day!

Reconciliation is not easy, but it is worth every ounce of effort it demands. Later in this chapter I want to present some practical guidelines that will make successful reconciliation more probable. Before I get to them, however, I want to look at two methods of dealing with anger that are neither God-honoring nor constructive. Taking an honest look at these commonly used approaches will enable us to be more appreciative of the wisdom of God's method for resolving anger.

Repression? Explosion?

One of the most common forms of dealing with anger, particularly for many Christians, is repression. When we begin to experience feelings of anger because of something that has taken place in a relationship, we think, "I shouldn't be angry about such a little thing. If I were as 'spiritually mature' as I claim to be, this wouldn't bother me at all." So we repress our feelings of anger, attempting to convince ourselves that they really don't exist. Others of us are more honest about our feelings, but still unwilling to deal with them openly. "Well, yes," we say, "I know I'm angry, but I just can't handle confrontation. I don't want to rock the boat. I don't want anybody to get hurt." In both cases, we shove our anger into the closet of our minds, only to let it fester into a cancer of hateful emotions.

Let me make one point of clarification before we go on. As a person grows in the Lord, he does, in fact, find that some mild irritations and minor relational conflicts can be dismissed with grace and even humor. In other words, because of the tenderizing work of the Holy Spirit in his life, he no longer gets angry about certain things that used to anger him. The irritation or conflict may cause some inconvenience, but it doesn't cause anger to take root.

When we see this fruit of maturity blossoming in our lives, we should thank God for it. It is because of His work in us that we are becoming more tolerant, patient, and forgiving. I mention this with caution, however, because it is so important that we are honest and careful in determining whether a certain irritation or conflict can successfully be dismissed from our minds, or whether our attempts to do so will lead to unhealthy repression. There is no merit in pretending that something doesn't bother us when in reality it does. The great problem with repression is that when we stuff an emotionally charged bout with anger into the closet, we're setting the stage for trouble. The closet can only hold so much. There will inevitably come a day when the closet door bursts open and the anger flies!

That brings us to the second most popular method of dealing with anger: the explosion method. As incredible as it seems, some psychologists (though fewer and fewer all the time) still advocate this method. "Let it fly," they say. "Get it all out of your system. Don't worry about restrictions and guidelines. Face the person who made you angry and tell him exactly how you feel. Let it rip!"

I can't begin to tell you how strongly I feel about the fallacy of this counsel. I call it the "explosion method." What happens when a bomb explodes? Think about it. What is left after the explosion? Well, there's shrapnel, broken glass, torn bodies, bits and pieces of life here and there. Fragments, that's all.

The same thing happens when we go to a family member or a friend and release a verbal explosion of anger. We're left with fragments, torn feelings, broken bonds, bits and pieces of a relationship. Before a God who is committed to glorifying Himself through the quality of our relationships, such destruction stands as a serious offense.

Before I made my stand on this subject public, I was frequently approached by people who wanted to impress me with their "guts." With a proud look of conquest in their eyes, they would say, "Wow, do I feel great! For four years I worked for a self-centered egomaniac and put up with his power plays and broken promises. But today I went into his office and told him just what I thought of him. I blistered him! I ripped him to shreds! You should have seen his face when I looked him straight in the eye and said, 'I quit! Do you hear that? I quit!' Then I slammed the door and walked out. Boy, did that feel good!"

Whether such encounters occur between family members, church members, neighbors, or employers and employees, my response is always the same. "Does what is left of that relationship bring honor to God? Is He pleased with what you've done?"

If we who are sincere believers allow ourselves to vent our anger in such a way that we destroy relationships, we are making a lot of extra work for ourselves. Why? Because if we mean business in our relationships with Christ, if we are serious about wanting to please Him, we are called to attempt to restore every relationship we have broken. And if we've just exloded in anger and blown a relationship to pieces, we're going to have to work awfully hard to put the pieces back together.

Hate Letters

Occasionally I receive letters from people who see me as the tangible symbol of all that they hate about church or Christians or God or Jesus Christ. These letters are filled with criticism and condemnation and unsubstantiated accusations. Now, as much as I hate to say this, I have a hard time handling these letters. In fact, sometimes when I read this kind of letter, my anger boils! I have an almost irrepressible desire to lick my pen, grab a piece of paper, and launch a verbal missile. How I long to say, "Look, buddy, pastors have feelings too. . . ." and proceed with an exposition of my opponents' obvious insensitivity and ignorance!

But I can't do it. There's always one thought that stops me just short of retaliation. I know that if I yield to my desire to avenge my anger, I'm going to have to pay a high price. Sooner or later the

Holy Spirit is going to convict me and ask, "Is there a broken relationship in your life right now? Leave your offering at the altar and go to attempt to restore it." At that point I will face the overwhelming task of putting together the tiny pieces of a relationship that was needlessly shattered. Is that worth the few moments of sinful satisfaction I enjoyed?

The point of these last few pages is this: God calls us to reconciliation. That is an indisputable fact. Given that fact, we need to ask ourselves a practical question. Do we want to face the near-impossible task of restoring a relationship that is torn into tiny fragments, or do we want to have a little more to work with than that? For myself, I choose the latter. If I explode in anger and blow a relationship to shreds, I will have to walk a hard road to reconciliation. It makes much more sense to me to find a way of expressing my anger that leaves clear the path to relational harmony.

Loving Confrontation

Repression doesn't work. Explosion causes too much damage. What's the alternative?

The Bible says that the acceptable pattern for resolving relational conflict centers around the concept of loving confrontation. From this point on, you may dislike this chapter. No one enjoys confrontation. We all wish for an easier way to deal with conflict. But the Bible says that when we have a conflict with another person, we must go to him and attempt to resolve the conflict through loving confrontation.

Matthew 5:23-24 makes it clear that when anger disrupts a relationship, we are obligated before God to *go to the other person and attempt a reconciliation*. It doesn't matter who is at fault. God doesn't care whether it's our anger or the other person's anger that is causing the division. If there is relational conflict, we must *go to the other person*. We are not given the freedom to sit back and wait for him to come to us. Nor are we permitted to go behind his back, discuss the situation, and compound the problem. We are to go directly to him, in private (Matt. 18:15), to begin the process of reconciliation.

The first step in the reconciliation process, after coming together in private, is to verbally affirm the relationship. Because of the tension, anger, and hostility in the relationship, a confrontation is necessary, but it must be preceded by affirmation. A great way to begin a reconciliation in a marriage is to say, "Honey, I love you and I want you to know how much this relationship means to me. I want this relationship to last forever and be pleasing to us and to God. That's why I want to solve this problem now."

If it becomes necessary to confront an employer, begin by saying, "I have to tell you that I'm angry about something, but before I do I just want to make sure that you know how much I enjoy working here. I value this job. I love what I'm doing, and I want to protect this vocation. I want you to understand this. I didn't come here to cause a problem, but rather to solve one, to resolve our differences so that we can maintain a good working relationship."

If you have a problem with a fellow worker say, "You know, I really appreciate working with you, but there's something I have to talk to you about, something that will help us to work together more comfortably."

If at times you find it hard to be sincere in your affirmation or if you don't really feel that the relationship in question is that important to you, remind yourself that your feelings about the relationship are not the prime consideration. Of far greater significance is what God thinks of it, and He thinks it's extremely important. Remember, He wants every relationship we have to glorify Him. Regardless of what we may feel about a given relationship, God values it. For His sake, then, we can affirm it.

Lynne and I have made it a point to begin every confrontation with verbal, loving affirmation. Now, whenever she sits down beside me and says, "You know, Bill, I really value you and the relationship we share," I know exactly what's coming. I'm in for a confrontation! But that's OK, because in the vast majority of cases, a discussion that begins with such an affirming statement ends with a constructive breakthrough that has a solidifying effect on any relationship.

The second step in the reconciliation process is so practical that some people will wonder why I even mention it. Others, however, will know all too well how important it is. The second step in this: guard your volume level. When a confrontation begins with loud, harsh words, it is almost sure to end in failure. "I'm sick and tired of you and your . . ." will only serve to fan the flames of hostility.

"A gentle answer turns away wrath, but a harsh word stirs up anger" (Prov. 15:1). These words of the wise King Solomon are as true today as they were the day they were written.

The third step in the process is to use "I feel" statements to express your anger. Most of us tend to express our anger through accusations. "I'm angry because you never get your reports in on time." "I'm angry because you're never home." "I'm angry because you didn't get the laundry done."

How do we respond when such accusations are hurled in our faces? We become defensive. We think, "Hey, I'm being attacked. I'd better protect myself!"

"How dare you say I never get the reports done on time? If you didn't overload me with work, I'd have them done on schedule every time!"

"What do you mean, 'I'm *never* home?' I'm home right now, aren't I? If you were a little more pleasant, I might spend even more time here."

"The laundry? How do you think I can get the laundry done with this stupid washing machine you bought? What do you think I am, superwoman?"

Accusations seldom lead the discussion to the root of the problem. They just start a verbal battle that no one wins. Accusations are traded as the volume level inevitably rises, and the relationship is more severely damaged than it was before the discussion started.

How can the discussion take a different course? By following the affirmation with a statement of feeling. "Honey, listen. I feel hurt. I'm embarrassed to tell you this, but I feel hurt because it seems to me that I'm about tenth on your priority list. Maybe I'm wrong, but that's the way I feel. Can we talk about this?"

If you're talking to your employer say, "I enjoy working here, but I feel that you take me for granted. Perhaps you don't, but that's how I feel. Now and then I start thinking that I'm just a number to you. As long as I do my job and don't rock the boat, you're happy with me, but I don't sense that you care for me as a person. I think I should have been involved in that decision. Maybe I'm wrong, but that's how I feel. Can we discuss this?"

While accusations increase hostility, the expression of feelings usually opens the way for a solution to the problem. Not infrequently Lynne has said to me, "Bill, I feel lonely. Even when you're with me I feel like I'm alone. It seems to me that you're preoccupied, that you're not really tuned in to me." If she were to lash out at me with obvious hostility and say, "Bill, what's wrong with you? Why don't you ever listen to me? Can't you be a little more sensitive?" I would probably respond defensively and toss back an equally harsh rebuttal. But when she approaches me with a sincere expression of her feelings, I am prompted to respond sensitively and seriously to her need. "OK, let's talk about this. You probably have good reason to feel that way. Let's take a closer look at what's going on during the time we spend together." With an opening like that, the conversation that follows is almost sure to be constructive and healing.

The catch to this entire process is that what we're really talking about at this point is self-disclosure, which is for most people (and particularly for men) extremely difficult. We can talk about a multitude of impersonal subjects with relative ease and fluency, but when it comes to disclosing our feelings, we're like tongue-tied schoolchildren.

Fortunately, the Bible offers us encouragement in this area. In Matthew 26:37-38, we read that Jesus "took with Him Peter and the two sons of Zebedee, and began to be grieved and distressed. Then He said to them, 'My soul is deeply grieved, to the point of death; remain here and keep watch with Me.'" In this passage we see a man, a leader, lay His heart bare before His friends and say, "Please listen to Me. I need to have someone understand how I feel. I'm so grieved about what is happening in this world and in My own life that I can barely stand up under the weight of the burden. Will you stay by Me and support Me? I need you."

Those tender words have freed me to be more open and honest about my feelings, my fears, and my needs. I have learned to say to Lynne, "You know, there are times when I just don't feel that I'm the man of God that I need to be. I get confused and tired and frustrated, and I wonder if God is even using me." Or I can say, "I feel like I'm so busy solving everybody else's problems that I never have time to consider my own. I always have to be the strong one, the leader, the man with the answers. Right now I need someone to take care of *me*. I need to know that there's someone watching out for *me*, supporting *me*. Please do that for me." Self-disclosure opens the door for meaningful communication, mutual understanding, and relational restoration.

Begin with affirmation. Guard your volume level. Use "I feel" statements. And now, establish resolves. After you share your feelings and identify the fundamental causes of the misunderstanding, the hurt, or the conflict, you can then ask the practical questions: "How can we avoid this particular problem in the future? How can we keep from hurting each other like this? What guidelines can we establish to keep us on a more positive track? Do we need a more formalized communication system in this office? Do we need more detailed job descriptions? Do we need a family calendar? Do we need to develop a more detailed family budget? In short, what practical steps can we take to avoid a future problem in this area?"

The preparatory steps are useless unless we move from them into this practical area of establishing resolves. A confrontation will have lasting results only if it leads to a workable plan for promoting relational harmony in the future.

The final step in the reconciliation process is to reaffirm the relationship. Self-disclosure may involve some painful exposure. Establishing resolves may involve a good deal of thoughtful creativity and compromise. After all that effort is invested in the relationship, it is time to say, "These times of difficulty will come and go. Anger will probably disrupt this relationship occasionally until the day we die. The evil one delights in destroying whatever gives God glory, including quality relationships. So let's commit ourselves right now to constructively working through these times of difficulty. You come to me. I'll go to you. Together, let's allow God to glorify Himself through us."

Affirm the relationship. Guard your volume level. Express your feelings. Establish resolves. Reaffirm the relationship. On paper these brief guidelines look easy, but in practice they will take every ounce of courage and discipline we can muster. Are we willing to be doers of God's Word, and not merely hearers?

As I look back over this chapter, I see that many of my remarks seem to be directed more at husband/wife relationships than at the relationships we have in the marketplace. I don't, however, feel too badly about this. The principles involved are the same in either case, and surely if we put them into practice in our homes first, we will be that much more able to practice them effectively in our workplaces. Besides, the family deserves to receive at least a minor benefit from this book on the marketplace!

My challenge to you is to take an inventory of your relationships. If there's a broken one, make an earnest attempt to restore it, the sooner the better. Commit yourself with renewed intensity to living in unity and peace with others. Swallow your sinful pride, and answer God's call to righteousness. Make every effort to glorify God in every relationship you have, whether it's in the family, the community, or the workplace. If you find yourself thinking that a given relationship is not worthy of the effort required for reconciliation, remind yourself of the value God places on it. His desire is that each and every relationship you have be permeated with peace and harmony.

Five

Profession or Obsession

Nearly 20 centuries ago, Jesus asked His disciples a question that continues to challenge the minds of thoughtful men and women. Recorded in Matthew 16:26, it reveals a wisdom far beyond the wisdom of this world, and an unparalled comprehension of economics and human values. With it Jesus cut to the core of man's quest for meaning, for fulfillment, for security, and for prosperity. He probed the thoughts that are pondered deep in the recesses of human hearts.

"For what will a man be profited," Jesus asked, "if he gains the whole world, and forfeits his soul?"

It's as if for a moment Jesus decided to speak the language of the marketplace. "Let's talk business," He said. "Let's talk profitability, bottom lines, net gains, whatever you want. I'm prepared. But let Me ask the first question. Is it good business to spend 60 years capturing all this world has to give, only to lose your very soul for eternity? Does that make sense? Think about it. What will your high achievements, your prestigious positions, your money, and your power do for you when your quota of earthly days is filled?"

In our businesses and secular organizations, we may be considered "key people," uniquely gifted in identifying the basic problems that jeopardize profitability and productivity. We may excel in the marketplace, becoming the presidents of companies, the chairmen of boards, the chief executives of corporations. We may be respected for our insight and perception of the realities of business.

55

But can we apply our practical business savvy to the larger matters of life and eternity? We know how to make the right choices in business; do we likewise know how to make the right choices in life?

Jesus takes the thought a step further. "Or what will a man give in exchange for his soul?" He asks (Matt. 16:26). "Let's talk trade. Let's talk values and comparisons. You have one soul. Is there anything worth trading for your soul? Anything?"

These are profound, even haunting words. Jesus seems to imply that there is a frequent connection between "gaining the world" (whatever that means to us) and neglecting the greater issues of eternity. We can't have it all. World conquering isn't easy. It may demand a high price, even our souls.

Not long ago an Olympic athlete spoke to the junior high students at our church. She repeated the theme expressed by so many other star athletes. "I trained six hours a day, seven days a week. I didn't have time for dating. I didn't have time for recreation. I didn't even do too well in school. But that's the way it had to be. If I wanted to earn a gold medal, I had to pay the price. Some things had to go."

With untiring effort and dogged determination, we can achieve great success in this world. *But it will cost something.* For many people it will cost them their health. A leading national news magazine called hypertension the secret killer of the American people. High blood pressure and heart attacks claim the lives of scores of success-seekers who don't have time to properly care for their bodies. For other people it will cost them their marriages and families. We need only look at the divorce rate of professionals to see the truth of this.

The price is indeed high. But Jesus says that's only the beginning. The loss of health and marriage and family is tragic; but infinitely more tragic is the loss of one's soul for eternity.

Luke 12 records Jesus' parable of the rich young fool. "The land of a certain rich man was very productive. And he began reasoning to himself, saying, 'What shall I do, since I have no place to store my crops?' And he said, 'This is what I will do: I will tear down my barns and build larger ones, and there I will store all my grain and my goods. And I will say to my soul, "Soul, you have many goods laid up for many years to come; take your ease, eat, drink and be merry"'" (vv.16-19). Here we see a picture of an already successful man who wants still more. He wants it all. He wants to keep pushing and striving and gaining. He wants to establish for himself an empire of wealth that will insure him a secure and happy future.

But the story didn't end according to his plan. In verse 20 God said to the man, "You fool! This very night your soul is required of you; and now who will own what you have prepared?" He was faced very suddenly with the dilemma of the man described in Ecclesiastes 2:18-19. "Thus I hated all the fruit of my labor for which I had labored under the sun, for I must leave it to the man who will come after me. And who knows whether he will be a wise man or a fool? Yet he will have control over all the fruit of my labor for which I have labored by acting wisely under the sun. This too is vanity." The rich young fool learned in an instant that the works of his hands held no guarantee for future security; neither did they ease his way into the life to come. Handing the fruit of his labors over to the people who followed him, he was forced to face God with empty hands and an empty heart.

Jesus ended the parable of Luke 12 with these words, "So is the man who lays up treasure for himself, and is not rich toward God" (v. 21). Jesus was saying, "You made a bad decision. It was no sin to build bigger barns, but it was the ultimate absurdity to neglect your soul. What a shame you never took the time to contemplate eternity, and establish for yourself a God-honoring empire of lasting treasure."

It amazes me that otherwise responsible men and women continue to make this same foolish choice. Even people who claim to be Christians persist in their attempts to gain the whole world, while day by day they experience the disintegration of their health, their marriages, their children, and their spiritual lives.

The Problem
Why do people continue to do this? Why did I do it for so many years? What drove me to "build the kingdom of God" while jeopardizing my own health, marriage, children, and spiritual life?

Part of the answer is that I, and many others like me, suffer from the illness of workaholism. Because of the faulty thought processes of our minds, we develop a dependence on overwork that has a noticeable adverse effect on the rest of our lives.

Some of us are so ill that we have equated our workaholic tendencies with the Protestant work ethic and we've made them a source of pride. We feel important when we have a frantic schedule, when we're overcommitted, when we're constantly running here and there, when we have beepers beeping, secretaries buzzing, and memos waiting to be produced. It makes us feel valuable. It proves our worth.

The disease of workaholism changes our professions into obsessions. It transforms our way of making a living into a way of life unto itself. Ordinary employment slowly takes on the characteristics of an unhealthy addiction.

Let me paint a portrait of the typical workaholic. Though I will use the male gender predominantly throughout this chapter, this picture could apply equally well to female workaholics. He is a perfectionist: neat, clean, orderly, dutiful, and conscientious. He is punctual, persistent, frugal, and reliable. He works hard and is good at tasks that require intense concentration. He is extremely competitive and needs to be in constant control of himself and those he is close to. He is extraordinarily self-willed and despises indecisiveness in himself and others. He has unrealistic expectations of himself and everyone else and avoids recognition of his own fallibility. In marriage he is careful to do his minimal share, yet he tries to do most of the thinking for his mate, and is stingy with his love and time. His conscience is overly strict, his thinking is rigid, and he often appears cold and intimidating. He expresses anger more easily than warmth because it encourages distance in interpersonal relationships. He generally keeps his feeling to himself, and attempts to intellectualize to avoid emotions. He frequently makes his accomplishments the subject of conversation.

The description could go on and on, but it can be summarized in the following way: The workaholic maintains a frantic schedule. He is consistently preoccupied with performance. He finds it difficult to refuse additional responsibilities. He is unable to relax.*

---

*For this profile and much of the information presented in this chapter, I am indebted to Dr. Paul Meier and his colleagues who wrote the excellent book, *The Workaholic and His Family,* published by Baker Book House, 1981. To anyone who suspects that he or she is a workaholic or may be married to one, I highly recommend this practical, informative book.

If someone you know exhibits these characteristics, he or she is probably a workaholic.

The Cause

Most people think that workaholics are driven by their desire to acquire more and more money, but in the majority of cases this is not true. Most experts on this subject agree that workaholics are driven not by greed, but by their deep-seated personal insecurity.

Generally speaking, this insecurity has its roots in childhood. As a child, he received too little encouragement, praise, and approval from his parents. Regardless of how well he performed in school, plays, sports, etc., he never seemed to do well enough. His parents were never satisfied. They always made him feel that he "could have done better." Consequently, he saw himself as a constant failure, never measuring up to his parents' expectations. He felt guilty because he couldn't please them, and grew up thinking that anything short of perfection was failure.

Because he learned early that his parents' love was conditional, dependent on the quality of his performance, he developed a performance-oriented lifestyle. He usually takes on more responsibility than he can comfortably handle; consequently his schedule is chronically overloaded and he's unable to relax. Though he works hard and usually does a good job at whatever he attempts, he is never satisifed. He always feels that he should have done better—or more. He is always frustrated and burdened by the guilt of being imperfect.

He is haunted by his low self-esteem, and though he appears to be strong, decisive, and positive, he is really desperately insecure and yearns to be respected and valued. He wants to be recognized as an important, successful individual, and he'll do anything to gain that recognition. He thrives on awards of excellence. He loves to set records. He spends the majority of his life working to amass wealth, power, and prestige in a futile attempt to convince himself that he is worth something. To borrow from a well-known television commercial, "He is driven!"

He may appear to other people to be the epitome of stability, dedication, and commitment. His efforts, however, are directed by his desperate need to cover his feelings of inferiority. His diligent work may be partially motivated by a sincere desire to establish a God-pleasing credibility on the job such as we discussed in chapter 2, but that is only a secondary consideration. He is far more concerned with making an impressive performance to achieve his own selfish ends.

While the workaholic frequently doesn't recognize his problem, others do, especially his spouse and children, who probably suffer more because of his illness than he does himself.

As a result of his conscientious work (and the 100 hours a week that he devotes to it!), the workaholic is usually successful in his career. Because of this success, he has the wherewithall to supply his family with ample material benefits. So, when his wife expresses her frustration with the state of their marriage and her desire for a more intimate, fulfilling relationship with him, he gives her his standard reply. Can you guess what he says?

"What do you expect from me? Most wives would give anything to own a house like this, to wear the clothes you wear, to drive the cars we drive, and take the vacations we take. What do you want from me? Won't you ever be satisfied?" Because he sees these "symbols of success" as the possible fulfillment of his needs for recognition and security, he expects his wife to see them that way too. When she doesn't, he convinces himself that she is selfish, unappreciative, and unloving.

The workaholic is famous for claiming his indispensability to his company or institution. When his wife expresses her need for more of his time, he says, "Oh, sure, I'll stay home tonight. But I just want you to know this will cost me my biggest account." How can a spouse respond to a statement like that? It doesn't even lay the groundwork for a fair fight. It does, however, reveal the depth of deception that clouds the mind of the workaholic. He deceives himself, his wife, and everyone close to him into believing that they have no claim on his time, his affections, or his efforts.

If the workaholic is in the people-serving professions—doctor, minister, etc.—this problem is compounded. He will blantantly use guilt-producing techniques in his attempt to diminish the validity of his spouse's requests. I was an expert at that. During the early years of our marriage, it was not uncommon for me to be out every night for three or four weeks at a time "building the ministry." Occasionally Lynne would say something innocent like, "Bill, why don't you stay home tonight? It has been so long since we've talked." I would look at her in utter disbelief and say, "Half the world is going to hell and you want me to sit home and hold your hand. You've got to be kidding! What kind of Christian are you? How dare you try to limit the mighty world-saver! You have no heart for people." Thank God Lynne had and still has the perception required to see through my faulty thought patterns and the strength of conviction and character required to confront me when needed. My self-centered blindness could have destroyed her and the potential for the meaningful relationship we now share.

It's true that we are called by God to work hard and conscientiously, but we are never called to work so hard that we neglect the basic responsibilities of family life. The children of workaholics get toys, bikes, trips, cars, and big allowances, but they are denied what they crave the most: time and love.

Kids today are crying out, "Dad, won't you play ball with me?" "Mom, won't you watch me in the school play?" "Won't you sit down and talk to me?" They're not asking for much. We don't have to drive them to school and eat lunch with them in the cafeteria and lead them through each and every step of their day. We just have to give them enough time and attention to convince them that they're as valuable to us as our biggest account or our closest business associate.

Because the workaholic often imposes his own strict standards on the rest of his family, his children receive his message of conditional love. They, like him, are afraid to fail, afraid that they will not receive his love. Often the children of a workaholic receive his praise for the awards or trophies they win, but they don't receive the individual, personal attention from him that would prove his appreciation of them as unique individuals. He doesn't take the time to watch their ball games or school plays, or listen to their recitals, or read the papers that they have so carefully written. He is concerned with the quality of performance, but not with the individual who has performed.

I am amazed at how often older adults talk about the "confused and irresponsible" young people of today. Sometimes I want to say, "Yes, they are confused and irresponsible, but if you'd take the time to look in the mirror, you'd see why they're that way." Many kids are driven to rebellious and irresponsible behavior in a last-resort attempt to get the attention they crave. They're longing to feel a sense of commitment from their parents. When they don't they experience anger, an anger provoked by a father or mother who is unwilling to take the time to love them.

The Apostle Paul admonishes, "Fathers, do not provoke your children to anger; but bring them up in the discipline and instruction of the Lord" (Eph. 6:4). It takes a commitment of time and emotional effort to show our kids that we love them and to teach them the discipline and instruction of the Lord. There's no other way to be obedient to the Word of God.

The Cure

The non-Christian experts offer a rainbow of options to the workaholic who wants to change. They range from dropping out of the marketplace altogether to attending workaholic therapy groups. I'm sure there is some merit to these suggestions, but I believe the Bible offers a far more fundamental, and therefore more effective way to cure the workaholic.

First, we must confront the workaholic with the Word of God. He must be forced to hear what God says about the root of his problem, personal insecurity. The way a child views his parents often affects the way he views God. Because the workaholic viewed his parents as those who only gave love on a conditional basis, he tends to view God the same way, as critical and unforgiving, seeing him as a constant failure. And just as he sought to gain his parents' approval through his performance and achievement, so he tries to merit God's love through his human efforts. He tries to earn God's love, acceptance, and forgiveness.

What the workaholic needs to know, then, is that God's love is not conditional. He doesn't have to earn it. It is not based on his performance or perfection, his "good works," to use the biblical term.

Remember Mary and Martha, who had the privilege of welcoming Jesus into their home? Mary was overwhelmed by the presence of the Lord and devoted herself to His teaching. She sat quietly at His feet and drank in every sip of living water that He offered. Martha, on the other hand, devoted herself to extravagant preparations which demanded all her time and energies. She wanted to prove to Jesus by the quantity of her work that she was worthy of

His approval and deserving of His love. Jesus, however, saw right through her frantic efforts to the insecurity that festered in her heart. "Martha, Martha," He said, "you don't have to prove your worth to Me. I love you just the way you are. Come, sit down. Share your time with Me, and listen to My words" (my paraphrase of Luke 10:41-42).

God graphically proved His love for us at the cross. "Greater love has no one than this, that one lay down his life for his friends" (John 15:13). That's exactly what God did for us. In the person of Jesus, He gave His life so that we might be redeemed from sin and live for eternity. Workaholics need to hear that over and over. God validated our worth at the cross. We need not concern ourselves with men's applause and cheap achievement awards. We have the approval and acceptance of the Lord of the universe.

The workaholic who is looking for security in the fruits of his labors must learn that ultimate security lies in a relationship with God, a relationship which is not earned, but rather accepted as a free gift. "But God, being rich in mercy, because of His great love with which He loved us, even when we were dead in our transgressions, made us alive together with Christ (by grace you have been saved), and raised us up with Him, and seated us with Him in the heavenly places, in Christ Jesus, in order that in the ages to come He might show the surpassing riches of His grace in kindness toward us in Christ Jesus. For by grace you have been saved through faith; and that not of yourselves, it is the gift of God; not as a result of works, that no one should boast" (Eph. 2:4-9). Even when we are dead in our transgressions, God offers us the gift of His love and His presence, through our faith in Christ Jesus. We don't work for it; we don't earn it. We simply accept, in gracious humility, God's offer to be united with us as a loving father is united with a son.

The workaholic is obsessed with gathering and storing up, with producing and performing. Only when he fully understands the love of God can he begin to give up his futile struggle to gain acceptance. When he realizes that he is significant because God declares him significant, he will be free to give up his attempts to prove his significance. He will also be free to enjoy his work.

In addition to learning that God loves him, the workaholic must learn that others love and accept him as well. The wife of a workaholic must affirm her love for him and express appreciation for his good qualities. She must also be patient with his faults, realizing that they stem from his deep insecurity. She must learn to positively reinforce behavior that is not work-related, and gently convince him that he, not his money or accomplishments, is what she values most. On the other hand, she must show reasonable appreciation for the material things he gives her, since this may be the only way he knows to show love. To reject them, therefore, would be to reject his love.

She must be careful too that she doesn't encourage his workaholic tendencies by being critical and unforgiving, as his parents were, or by being overly dependent on him, expecting him to meet all her emotional needs. Still, she must learn to communicate her needs and opinions in an honest, God-honoring way that will gradually and gently encourage the type of genuine intimacy which is crucial to a good marriage.

The next chapter provides some practical guidelines for sensible, God-pleasing scheduling, but before we go on to that I feel compelled to make one additional reference to the words of Matthew 16:26 which opened this chapter. If you have been so preoccupied with gaining the world that you've never taken the time to turn to the Saviour, please let the words of Jesus touch your heart and mind. "For what will a man be profited, if he gains the whole world, and forfeits his soul? Or what will a man give in exchange for his soul?"

Right now you can respond to these words. You can admit your sinful condition to God and turn to Christ for forgiveness and acceptance. If you know that you are driven by personal insecurity, immerse yourself in the knowledge that God loves you just as you are. He is willing and waiting to claim you as His beloved child.

Six

Scheduling for Sanity

You can't believe it! You've never won anything before in your life. You barely remember filling out the registration card as you left the store a few months ago. And now your name has been drawn!

You have been selected to participate in the "Thirty-Minute Madness Special." That's right. You have been given 30 minutes to race up and down the aisles of the store and fill your cart with as much food as you can. In fact, you can fill as many carts as you want. And then you get to take it all home—without paying a penny! It's a once-in-a-life-time opportunity.

You should be thrilled. At this very moment the store manager is informing the minicam crew that there are just three minutes left before your shopping spree begins. But you're not thrilled. You're actually a little sick to your stomach. Your palms are sweating as you tighten your grip on the grocery cart. You're just beginning to realize how grossly unprepared you are for this adventure. Your vision is blurred by the thousands of items lining the shelves from floor to ceiling, aisle after aisle.

Where do you begin? You blush inside because you know you had ample time to plan your strategy. Why didn't you put together a long-term family menu? Or make a list of your favorite large ticket items, like meat and specialty products? Why didn't you make an aisle chart to help you remember where each department was located?

You could have done so many things to maximize this opportuni-

65

ty. But you didn't take the time. You didn't think it through, and now the manager is about to give the signal to begin. The TV lights go on, and the people cheer. But in your heart you feel sick. You're winging it, and you know it. You're about to waste a once-in-a-lifetime opportunity!

Our Vision Is Blurred

How like that frustrated shopper we are as we face the shelves lined from floor to ceiling with a multitude of beautiful opportunities begging for our time. Our vision is blurred by the sheer volume of worthwhile activities available to us, all wrapped in brightly colored packages just waiting to be claimed.

The problem is that we have an infinite number of opportunities, but a finite amount of time. There are 1,440 minutes in a day, 168 hours in a week, and 52 weeks in a year. How do we decide where to invest our time? Where do we begin?

We begin by looking at the biblical view of time and understanding the value that God places on it. "As for the days of our life, they contain 70 years, or if due to strength, 80 years, yet their pride is but labor and sorrow; for soon it is gone and we fly away. . . . So teach us to number our days, that we may present to Thee a heart of wisdom" (Ps. 90:10, 12). When we're young we think that life is long, but as we age we realize that our years are few. The time is short that we have to prepare our hearts to meet our God. Time is valuable, therefore, because it is limited.

Jesus said, "We must work the works of Him who sent Me, as long as it is day; night is coming, when no man can work" (John 9:4). Here, as in the Psalms, the Word of God emphasizes the limited nature of time. Each of us has a limited amount of time to invest for eternity. There will come a day when our opportunities to work will be gone.

I remember so well working on the farm near our home in Kalamazoo during the summers of my high school years. During the peak season, we would get up at the break of day to begin planting or harvesting. We would continue working the fields until it was so dark we could barely see the rows. We even tried hitching lights to the equipment to extend the hours of our workday. We had to maximize the time. The days seemed so short, and there was so much work to be done.

Our Time Is Limited

Mindful that we ought to live each day of our lives with that same urgency, we ought to be constantly aware that we have a limited amount of time to invest in the kingdom of God. Every Christian leader who has had a significant impact on my life has exhibited this sense of urgency. One of these men, the executive director of an international youth organization, used to say to me, "Bill, I just don't know how much time I have to work with these kids. They grow up so quickly and then they go their own way." Even now when he talks with me, his parting words always reiterate the same theme: we don't know how much time we have left. "Teach the Word of God, Bill," he says. "Don't neglect your calling. The time is short."

In a world which places such an existential value on time, it is uncommon to hear someone put such a premium value on it, yet that is what God does. He reminds us that time is limited and He instills within us a godly sense of urgency. He also tells us that we will be held accountable for the way we use the time we have been given. In Colossians 4:5 Paul says, "Conduct yourselves with wisdom toward outsiders, making the most of the opportunity." Again in Ephesians 5:15-16 he says, "Therefore be careful how you walk, not as unwise men, but as wise, making the most of your time, because the days are evil." The time we have is a sacred trust from God. We are called to use it wisely, as good stewards.

Concerning Money

Later in this book we will look more at what the Bible says about our money, but I want to make just a brief comment about it here. We as believers must come to the ultimate understanding that everything we have is the Lord's, that we are merely managers of the material and monetary resources that we hold in our possession. We are not the owners, but rather the stewards, and someday we will face a "heavenly audit" to determine how well or how poorly we have managed that with which we were entrusted. Did we hoard our money? Did we squander it carelessly? Did we spend it selfishly? Did we invest it wisely? Did we support God's work generously? Did we tithe faithfully? One day we will be called to give account of the way we used our material resources.

About Time

What few people seem to understand is that the same is true of our time. We will be called to give account of how we used our time. Why? Because what we call "our time" is not really ours, but God's. It is a gift which He has given us to manage, to use for His glory. It is vital, therefore, that we learn to make the proper choices, to determine the best ways to use our time.

God calls us to make the most of our time, but He doesn't call us to overschedule ourselves to the brink of insanity. That is why we must learn to eliminate those activities which do not please Him (or are not priorities with Him), so we will have the time to do the things that do please Him (which are high priority to Him).

What makes it so hard to address this issue is that most of the people I know who live with insane schedules have *not* filled their time with worthless activities. On the contrary, they are involved in multitudes of worthwhile activities. In my own church, for example, I see hundreds of people who dedicate themselves to godly and justifiable projects that expand the ministry of the body of Christ in numerous ways. The problem is that even though these people are overscheduled with *great* activities, they are overscheduled nonetheless. They are so overscheduled that husbands and wives wave to one another as they pass each other going different directions on the church entry road. I've even heard that there's a bounty on the heads of available baby-sitters in our church!

As admirable as this problem sounds, in that it indicates hearts that are warm toward God and His people, it is a problem that must be solved. The toll that it takes is awesome. It destroys people physically. It fragments marriages and families. And ultimately it inhibits relationships with God.

Why do I feel so strongly about this subject that I am devoting two chapters of this book to it? Because it has been such a problem for me, personally. In the previous chapter I admitted that I was a workaholic, and believe me, that was no empty admission given for the sake of writing style or to make a surface-level identification with my readers. Today I have a balanced, God-honoring schedule, but in the past my family and I both suffered the very real effects of insane scheduling.

In preparing for this chapter I have tried to determine just what it was that brought me from the point of chronic overscheduling to where I am now. What prompted the gradual transformation? During the past weeks I have reflected at length on the past few years in an attempt to understand exactly what happened and why it happened. The remainder of this chapter is the result of that personal analysis.

Seven years ago I reached the peak of my personal insanity with respect to my schedule. At that time I was a youth minister at a church that had a very successful and active youth program. On Sunday mornings at 8:00 I had a weekly planning session with all the youth coordinators. At 9 I taught a Sunday School class. At 11, I led a portion of the adult church service. In the afternoon I had a music rehearsal and on Sunday evening I had to attend another church service. That was the set schedule for every Sunday.

On Monday evening I taught a Bible study to 450 high school students, the core group of our high school program. On Tuesday evening I directed a program for third-, fourth-, and fifth-grade boys which involved 125 kids and approximately 20 leaders. On Wednesday night I taught a Bible study at Son City, our high school outreach ministry, which involved 600 students. On Thursday night I taught an identical Bible study to another 500-600 high school kids. (The church sanctuary was not large enough to hold the entire Son City group, so we ran two identical programs.) On Friday night I spent time with various leaders in the high school ministry, and on Saturday I prepared for the following week's messages.

Those were the fixed events that took place every week. All during that time I was a full-time student at Trinity College, taking a minimum of 16 hours each semester, I was married (at least on paper), Lynne was pregnant and sick, and we lived in a tiny two-bedroom house with two adult boarders who we were attempting to "establish in the faith" and four dogs.

That describes the peak of my personal insanity. If anyone reading the last few paragraphs thinks that I am speaking out of pride, or boasting of my ability to handle a heavy schedule, please read those paragraphs again. Could *anyone* be proud of such a ridiculous and selfish schedule? On the contrary, it is with embarrassment that I share those years. Lynne deserves a purple heart for what she endured during that time. I didn't know then but I know now how severely I wounded her, and not only her, but many other people as well.

During that time I heard many messages on "priorities," and on "the barrenness of the busy life," and I felt a certain amount of pressure from Lynne and other people who warned me about the dangers of my chronic overscheduling. But the messages and the counsel had little effect on me because they both seemed to elevate the easy life, the balanced life, the comfortable life. And that seemed so contrary to what I saw in the lives of David and Paul and Peter and Jesus. These men were zealots. They had an internal intensity that burned. These heroes of the faith didn't lead the easy life, and I didn't want to either.

I didn't realize at that time that there is a law of diminishing returns in relation to personal scheduling. I didn't know then that there comes a point when our efforts become counterproductive, when our "busyness" actually limits our fruitfulness. Had I known that, perhaps I would have slowed down, but I didn't, I was still caught up in a thought system that perpetuated my desire to work harder and harder, and longer and longer, in an attempt to live a life that would be pleasing to God.

My "Slow-down"

What was it then that ultimately spurred the gradual transformation in my schedule, if it was not the "slow-down" messages and the external pressure? It was, quite simply, the Word of God. I can honestly say that all during that time of insane scheduling, I loved the Lord with all my heart, and I committed myself to spending time in prayer and in reading the Bible every day, no matter how crazy my schedule was. I was also committed to being a part of a church body where I could hear biblical teaching and be shaped by the fellowship of other Christians. As I just said, I wasn't yet ready to listen to the "slow-down" messages or heed the counsel of those who condemned my personal schedule; those words I completely ignored. But there were other words of Scripture and words of counsel that I did listen to, and they eventually provided the punch that knocked some sense into the head of this stubborn-willed Dutchman. Gradually, the Holy Spirit of God worked through the Word of God to shape my values, my attitudes, and ultimately, my schedule.

I'll never forget the morning that I woke up early to spend some time studying Ephesians 5. I started my quiet time that morning with a brief time of praise and thanksgiving. "O Lord, I love You and I thank You for Your death on the cross and the eternal salvation that You have given me. I want my life to give You glory. Right now help me to feed on Your Word and apply it to my life. Amen."

Then I opened my Bible to Ephesians 5:25 and read, "Husbands, love your wives, just as Christ also loved the church and gave Himself up for her." Those words hit me like a bolt of lightning and I knew I was in trouble! Up to that point I had been content to be a "good husband," and I had defined a good husband as one who was faithful to his wife and provided well for his family. Well, I had never been unfaithful to Lynne and I was certainly a good provider. We had a house. We had all the food and clothing we needed. The bills were paid on time. We had invested our money wisely. I was stable. I was consistent. Anyway I looked at it, I was a *good husband!*

But what I learned in that verse was that God wasn't satisfied with my being a "good husband." He wanted me to be a godly husband; there is a big difference between the two.

Paul tells us to love our wives as Christ loved the church. Did Christ impatiently tolerate the church and make excuses for His preoccupation with other things? Certainly not! His preoccupation *was* the church. He was dedicated to its growth and nurture and total well-being. He was willing to give Himself up for it.

God's Word says that men are to love their wives in that same way. To a man who was accustomed to giving his wife last place on his priority list, these words cut. They called for a relationship characterized by tenderness and communication and service. They called me to be willing to "give myself up" for her in tangible, practical ways that would give evidence to my Christlike love for her.

As I read and reread this verse, I became convinced that God was calling me to make a radical change in my schedule. That was the only way I could honor His command to love Lynne. I had to give her my time. And over the years I have made that radical change. I am now convinced that I have to spend at least three, and preferably four nights a week at home and set aside all day Monday to spend with my family. I'm kidding myself if I think I can build a godly marriage or be a godly father with a lesser time commitment than that.

The interesting thing is that I have lost nothing in making this commitment to my family. In all truth, I have probably received more benefit from it than they have. A woman who is loved, encouraged, and nurtured by her husband is a joy to live with. She is a tender, loving, supportive companion. Likewise, children who are loved and affectionately attended to by their father respond with joyful, giving hearts.

James Dobson, the noted authority on the family, claims that the average middle-class father spends 37 seconds a day with his small children. I doubt if I spent that much time with my kids before the Lord turned my thinking upside down. There were just too many other things to do, too many people to attend to, too many needs to meet.

The only answer was to learn to say no. Now, when people call and request evening counseling sessions, or ask me to attend a meeting or accept an outside speaking engagement, I say, "Let me check my schedule." If they have requested time on a night that I have already set aside for family-time I say, "No, I'm sorry. I have an appointment that night." Little do they know that it's an appointment with Lynne and the kids! That "appointment" may mean nothing more than a quiet evening at home where I lie on the floor to be a "ramp" for Todd's trucks or I sit in a kitchen chair to be a "pretend student" in Shauna's "pretend school." If that's what it takes for me to honor God in my family life, that's what I'll do.

Not long ago our church showed the James Dobson film series "Focus on the Family" (from which I got the "37 second" information). Those of us on the church staff strongly recommended the films to all the parents in our church and many responded by committing themselves to seeing all of the films. However, I was appalled at the number of people, particularly men, who said to me, "Well, Bill, I know I need this series—my family life sure isn't what it should be—but I have a really busy week coming up. This is our peak season at work." Others said, "Oh, I'm sure they would be helpful, but I have a big hunting trip to get ready for. I just can't spare the time right now." Still others said, "I'd come, Bill, but I have tickets to the Bears' game. You know what a fan I am!"

There were so many "good" excuses, and in the past I would have been sympathetic. I would have said, "Oh, sure, I know you have to keep things under control at work." Or, "Sure, I understand. It takes a lot of time to plan a good trip. Have a great time!" Or, "I know how much you enjoy those pro games. Don't miss your chance."

Choose the "Best"

But my thinking has changed. I don't "understand" anymore. Sure, there are plenty of exciting, worthwhile opportunities "out there" calling for our attention, but are they the *best* things that we can do with our time? I would be a fool to say that we shouldn't devote a certain amount of our time to our work, our friends, and our recreation. But when an extraordinary opportunity to build the quality of our family life comes along, we should make that a priority. I found it hard to believe that these men could not offer even a few hours of their time to an activity that was sure to have a long-lasting, positive effect on their entire families and provide a stimulating challenge to their roles as fathers. We need to think less about filling our schedules with insignificant activities, and think more about what it means to honor God in our marriages and families.

The church is my career and for many years I laid myself down on the altar of my work, sacrificing my health, my wife, and my kids. It was not, however, a sacrifice that pleased the Lord. Again, the Holy Spirit had to speak to me through the Word of God. "For the body [the church] is not one member, but many" (1 Cor. 12:14). The Holy Spirit convicted me that I had been placing too much emphasis on myself, nurturing the egocentric view that if I didn't "get the job done," no one would.

I had to realize that I was responsible to God to use my spiritual gifts willingly and effectively, but that was as far as I was called to go. I was not called to take on responsibility that was not suited to my gifts and abilities, nor was I called to be chronically overloaded with commitments and responsibilities that jeopardized my health, my family, and my commitment to the Lord.

What about you? Have you laid your life down on the corporate altar? Do you say, "Well, yes, I know I'm ruining my family life, but what can I do? It's my job. I can't afford to lose my job." But can you afford to lose your family? Do you say, "Yes, I know it's tough on my marriage. But I make good money." You will have to do some pretty fancy footwork through Scripture to find any biblical justification for allowing your job to cause the disintegration of your marriage and family relationships. It just isn't there. Your profession may be, and should be a very worthwhile and gratifying endeavor, but your walk with the Lord, your marriage, and your family are of far greater significance.

I know what it means to be overscheduled to the point of absurdity. I also know, however, that the pattern of overscheduling can be broken. The first step in breaking the pattern is to sincerely commit your life to the Lord. Submit to Him daily. Thank Him for forgiving you and cleansing you. Acknowledge His authority in your life, and commit your time to Him.

The second step is to commit yourself to the public study of the Word of God. Commit yourself to being in Bible class and church services as often as you can. Then be willing to apply the truths of Scripture that you have learned.

The third step is to commit yourself to the private reading of the Word of God. Each day select a portion of Scripture and study it, internalize it, and obey it. Modern language Bibles and commentaries are readily available to aid you in your understanding of Scripture. This commitment of time and effort is guaranteed to open the floodgates of eternal rewards.

Seven

The Christian Consumer

Most Christians earnestly pray for God to guide them into the career that will best use their talents and bring them pleasure and satisfaction. Then they pray for the strength to pursue that career with diligence, for the perseverance to continue in spite of difficulties and setbacks, and for the wisdom and skill that will lead to advancement. However, when God graciously answers these prayers and blesses their efforts so that they are rewarded with financial gain, they all too often pocket their paychecks and say, "It's mine—all mine, *I* worked for it, *I* sacrificed for it, *I* claim it. Now *I* will enjoy it in any way *I* choose. *It's mine!*"

The Bible teaches from cover to cover that obedience to Christ involves yielding to Him the totality of our lives. It demands that we say, "Here I am. Here is my life. Here are my sins, my assets and my liabilities, my strengths and my weaknesses. They're Yours. Take all that I am and have and mold it into conformity with Your will."

Possessions and Personal Finances

Most believers are willing to surrender to God their broken relationships, their frustrated ambitions, and a host of other sin-related problems that make all too obvious their need for God's absolute forgiveness and His divine power. But few believers are really willing to surrender to Him their possessions and their personal finances; these they cling to as their right, their security, and their just reward.

75

Perhaps that is why personal finances are the cause for concern and anxiety for so many Christians. One of the leading causes of discord, even divorce, among young married couples is financial incompatibility. Financial frustration leads to tension, which in turn leads to the gradual disintegration of communication, and ultimately to the collapse of the marriage.

Many people, including Christians, appear to have a casual, almost irresponsible attitude toward their financial difficulties. "I'm a step ahead of the creditors. I'm keeping the wolves away," they say. "If I change addresses often enough, they'll never catch me!" We could laugh at these words if only the frustration and fear they attempt to veil were not so clearly obvious. These casual responses are ineffective cover-ups.

The truth is that far too many Christians have allowed their personal finances to fall into shambles. They are deep in debt, with no means of handling unexpected expenses, and no practical plan for improving the situation. They are hopelessly caught in a never-ending circle of unpaid bills and unmet deadlines.

I see three major factors that have contributed to this problem. First, few pastors teach the biblical principles concerning finances. Seminary students are given reams of detailed information on theology, but virtually no information on finances, and few ministers ever have the opportunity to gain "on-the-job" financial experience or expertise. Consequently, they are unable to adequately address this subject.

Second, the public education system in this country tends to ignore the *basics* of personal financing. Though I had a business minor in my undergraduate work and learned the theories of microeconomics and macroeconomics, I never heard a classroom instructor explain how to balance a checkbook! I had to learn that "on the streets," so to speak. The same is true of banking and insurance and CDs and stocks and bonds and T-bills. Without the painstaking explanations of friends with financial expertise, I wouldn't know a thing about these very basic elements of finance. There's simply no convenient avenue through which we can obtain this information.

The third reason that many Christians are in financial difficulty is that in Christian circles information about personal finances is kept secret from even the most trusted friends. It's possible for most people to talk about marriage problems, health problems, and even spiritual problems, but *not* personal finances!

Isn't that strange? Financial difficulties are a major source of anxiety for many sincere Christians; yet we in the church have adopted an unofficial oath of silence on the subject, an oath which must be broken if we have any hope of alleviating the problem. Pastors must begin to teach the biblical principles that pertain to finances (or engage Christian financial experts to do so for them); schools must be encouraged to teach students the fundamentals of personal financing; and we must begin to open our hearts to one another about our own financial concerns.

It's God's Money

The money that we earn is not really *our* money. It is *God's* money, which He has merely entrusted to our management. That's why it is so important that we become better informed about financial matters and wiser in the handling of our earnings. We are not free to squander God's money through undisciplined, self-centered spending or through carelessness or lack of knowledge. Rather, we are called to be responsible, disciplined, and godly in the handling of our finances, closing our eyes and ears to the messages of an irresponsible society and making our financial decisions on the basis of sound biblical principles.

The remainder of this chapter is intended to alert the Christian consumer to the dangers of living in a materialistic society which beckons him to use God's money in ungodly ways.

Deceitful Advertising

Need I tell you that the advertising industry in America is a multi-billion dollar business? We are bombarded daily with hundreds of urgent messages in radio and TV commercials, newspaper ads, magazines, billboards, neon signs, mailings, matchbooks, bumper stickers, even dinnertime promotional phone calls. (Whenever a dinnertime caller greets me with a sweet-sounding voice and a blatant mispronunciation of "Hybels," I know I'm in for a smooth sales pitch!)

From the time we get up till the time we go to bed, we are battered with the same basic message. Buy this! Try that! Go there! Drink this! Smoke that! Watch me! Gradually the sheer volume of the advertising input wears down our defenses. Either we begin to believe the pitches, or we decide to buy the products just to silence the never-ending stream of voices begging for our responses.

In addition to pressure exerted by the sheer *volume* of advertising propaganda, we are also faced with the *seductive nature* of such propaganda. How many of us would be tempted to eat at a restaurant advertised on a billboard with a simple black and white block-letter message, giving the name, location, and a brief description of the type of cuisine served? We probably wouldn't give it a second thought. But what we actually see, in glorious living color on our television screens, is an enormous steak oozing and sizzling and crying out, "Eat me! Eat me!" The lure of the steak is exceeded only by the tantalizing call of the crab legs swimming in melted butter and lemon juice. As the lemon is squeezed in dramatic slow motion, a mellow, inviting voice adds the final tempting touch.

You know as well as I do that it's not easy to be content with last night's leftovers after having visually feasted on sizzling steak and crab legs. It takes awesome willpower not to get in the car and head for the advertised restaurant!

Advertisers play on our emotions in an attempt to seduce us into buying their products. What man can resist the promotional material of a car that is draped with a wild animal and a Playboy bunny? Or who can ignore the haze-hidden sports cars flying with Lear jets through billowy puffs of clouds, or the ice-glazed luxury sedans perched high on the peaks of majestic snowcapped mountains, or positioned delicately on the decks of sleek ocean liners, touched by the glistening spray of the tossing waves?

Scenes like that make me want to run outside and throw rocks at my '78 Chevy. And there's nothing wrong with my Chevy! It runs fine, the interior is clean, an there's not a trace of rust on the body—not even a dent or scratch worth mentioning. But it's not emotional enough. Its four doors, whitewall tires, and automatic transmission make me feel more like an old man than a Lear jet pilot. I need something new and sleek and sporty! Do you see how seduction works?

As if the volume and seductive nature of advertising aren't enough, we must also be exposed to the out-and-out *deception* of advertisers. In preparing for this chapter, I read a fascinating book entitled *The Permissible Lie*, authored by Samm Sinclair Baker, and published by Beacon Press, Boston. Mr. Baker worked in the advertising industry for 30 years before choosing to leave the profession. In his book, he exposes the deceptive advertising produced by the inner circles of some of the nation's largest advertising agencies. On page 14 he says, "To increase sales, most anything goes—misrepresentation, deception, lies—unless actionable. The approach is usually to produce the hardest-selling campaign without perpetrating recognizable fraud." Fraud, lies—they're fine, as long as you don't get caught. On page 25 he continues:

In a typical meeting, an advertiser told agency men: "Our top canned item is slipping. We need some new excitement in the advertising. We're going to redesign the label to give it a new look. So come up with a 'New! Improved!' campaign—lots of big-big promises. Show us layouts in a week so we can move fast."

Someone asked, "Anything new or improved *inside* the can?"

The client glared. "What . . . kind of a question is that? I'd have said so if we'd made any changes other than the label. That'll be redesigned and the product will *look* new and improved, won't it? Whose side are you on anyhow?"

The questioner wasn't on any side very long. He was fired from the agency.

Mr. Baker summarizes his conclusions after 30 years' experience on page 5:

First, the overwhelming aim of advertising is to make a profit; to serve the public best becomes a secondary consideration and is confined within the limits of the profit motivation. A lie that helps build profits is considered a permissible lie. Of course, the lie must not be so blatant that it results in eventual damage to the company's profits.

Second, a substantial amount of advertising is based on the concept of the permissible lie.

Third, this fakery, through saturation and repetition, undermines the attitudes and ethics of the adult, the child, and the family.

Fourth, and highly important, I am convinced that the immoral concept of the permissible lie is not necessary to achieve the improved sales and profits the advertiser demands.

Jesus said to His followers, "Behold, I send you out as sheep in the midst of wolves; therefore be shrewd as serpents, and innocent as doves" (Matt. 10:16). Christian consumers must learn to be less gullible. We must be wise as serpents, constantly examining and judging what is being presented to us as truth. Lynne and I enjoy pointing out to one another the other side of the picture—the reality side—that is usually not presented by advertisers. One of our "favorites" is the beer commercial which pictures a ruggedly handsome man in a classic leisure suit sliding down from the seat of a gleaming semitrailer that sports chrome wheels that have obviously never seen a dusty road. The distant sunset is spectacular, and as the driver saunters into the tidy tavern with the red plaid tablecloths, he is warmly greeted by old friends who offer him a tall, refreshing glass of beer. What a perfect way to end a long day.

But why, we wonder, doesn't the ad picture the handsome driver getting drunk and climbing back into his rig and swerving down the highway to smash into the back of a station wagon carrying a vacationing family? Why doesn't it show him going home and threatening his wife and kids as they cower fearfully in the corner, hoping against hope that this time they can escape his drunken anger? Why doesn't it show the morning after?

We must learn to look through what is presented to us in the media, until we can see clearly the unpictured reality. When I see cars flying through the clouds, I have to remind myself that these cars have payment books as thick as my Bible. I don't need that. My Chevy is paid for, and I never want to get back into the payment trap. I have to keep reminding myself of that.

In addition to learning to see the unpictured reality, we have to develop a spiritual cynicism in regard to advertising. We can't believe the results of every "research study" that is cited by promoters. Research results and statistics can be used or misused to prove almost anything.

We also have to learn to ask ourselves simple questions. Is it really so important that I own five pairs of designer jeans? Will I feel all that much better and more energic if I buy a new mattress for my bed? Will my daughter truly be happier if she has a doll that gets diaper rash? Will my marriage automatically be enriched by a Caribbean cruise? Advertisers would like us to answer yes to all these questions, and many more, but we can't allow ourselves to be that easily deceived. We are intelligent human beings, and we ought to have the courage to think accordingly!

To those of you reading this book who are in the advertising business, I can only say that I am aware of the difficulty of your position. I'm sure that more than once in my produce business days, I described a load of aging lettuce as "gorgeous as diamonds, fresh as the morning dew." I felt that I had to in order to make a sale, but I look back at that era of my life with shame, unable to justify my lies. I challenge you to examine your own promotions with eyes enlightened by the Word of God.

Easy Credit

The danger of deceitful advertising is given its power to ensnare us by a second danger, easy credit. Several thousand years ago the writer of Proverbs wrote, "The borrower becomes the lender's slave" (22:7). How the divine wisdom of that ancient author speaks to us today!

It's hard to believe the number of Christian people I talk with who are strapped financially. If they miss one or two paychecks, they are in serious financial trouble. They're mortgaged so deeply and indebted to so many people that if they incur one unexpected expense, they have to start sending letters of explanation to creditors.

So many of these people admit that they feel trapped, enslaved. And, in fact, they are. They have sold themselves to the lender. Proverbs 22:7 describes their lives perfectly.

How does indebtedness most frequently gain such control? The answer is *credit cards,* the plastic people-eaters! Daily, unsuspecting victims fall prey to their clutches. It is estimated that families with credit cards spend an average of 26 percent more per year than families without credit cards. It's no wonder that store owners will sacrifice 5 percent of each sale to cooperate with Mastercard and VISA. It's so simple for consumers to buy now and pay later. So simple.

But when young married couples find themselves facing mortgages, two car payments, appliance payments, furniture payments, clothing payments, and minimum monthly payments on gas cards and bank cards, it no longer looks so simple. In fact, it's often overwhelming.

"Owe nothing to anyone except to love one another" (Rom. 13:8). The principle behind this verse is that we should owe no one anything, except, of course, as we voluntarily offer ourselves, our services, or our resources to one another for the sake of love. To give ourselves to one another as a result of the love which Christ plants in our hearts for our brothers and sisters is not only permissible, but inevitable for true Christians. However, to indebt ourselves to others by unnecessary borrowing is wrong.

To qualify that principle, let me add that some indebtedness does seem to be reasonable and prudent in this society. Home mortgages, for example, are necessary for most families, and are, generally speaking, an acceptable debt, assuming of course that the mortgagee can afford the payments. Real estate is generally considered to be a good investment, not only because it appreciates in value, but also because the money invested can always be redeemed by the mortgagee, should that become necessary. Even here, however, a caution must be given. It is so easy for a young family to assume mortgage payments that are far too high for them to handle comfortably. They justify their action with the knowledge that a house is an appreciating item and a good investment, but they nonetheless become painfully strapped financially. A "good investment" is no longer good when it places undue strain on the investor.

Automobiles too are a major purchase that can have a substantial effect on any budget. Most families today accept at least one car payment as inevitable. Such thinking can, however, be dangerous. A car is a depreciating item; its full purchase price can seldom be redeemed. Therefore, unless our present vehicle is beyond use and beyond repair, we should make every effort to wait, plan, and save until we can pay cash for a new one. For many people, this is an important step in breaking the needless cycle of indebtedness.

Remember, money borrowed for depreciating items can never be redeemed. What is clothing worth once it is purchased and worn? What is the resale value of furniture? Christians must make a priority of becoming free from debt incurred for nonappreciable items if they want to safeguard the money that God has entrusted to their care.

Not long ago Lynne and I reached a mutual agreement that we would no longer use credit cards. We had not seriously jeopardized our financial standing, nor had we strapped ourselves into excessively high payments; we simply decided that we wanted to avoid *all* debt for depreciating items. We felt we could best do that by refraining totally from using credit cards. As a result of this decision, we have learned to plan ahead, to budget, to save, and to make wise choices. We now experience an even greater freedom in knowing that our spending is completely under control. We never spend money that we don't have.

Before we move into the next section of this chapter, I want to mention something that is purely a personal opinion, but I think it's worthy of some serious thought. I get nervous when I hear people talking about going shopping "just to look around," or "because there's nothing better to do," or "just for the fun of it." I can't help but ask myself, "Why would people do that? Aren't they aware of the dangers?"

Not far from my house there's a huge enclosed shopping center called Woodfield Mall. Busloads of people from miles around go to Woodfield to shop for everything from clothes to furniture to sporting goods. Certainly many of these people intend to do nothing more than casual "window shopping," but I wonder how many are really able to resist the temptation to buy.

If a person with a weakness for "sweets" goes window shopping at a Fannie May Candy Shop, chances are pretty good that he'll buy a chocolate bar and eat it. If a person with a "buying problem" (and most of us fit into that category) walks past the hundreds of stores at Woodfield Mall, chances are he too will buy one or more items and take them home.

When Lynne and I go shopping, we know what we need, we have a list, and we use it. When I need two spark plugs for my motorcycle, I go to the nearest Harley-Davidson shop, buy my spark plugs, and leave. If I stand around "admiring" the latest Harley accessories too long, I begin to hear them calling. "We need to be on your motorcycle!" they say. Once I hear that, I know I'm not far from yielding to temptation!

Undisciplined Budgeting

Get out of debt. Borrow only for items that appreciate in value. Pay cash for everything else. Ignore your credit cards. Does that sound unnecessarily dramatic to you? Perhaps it will sound a little less harsh if we focus our thoughts on the joy of being free from financial bondage and enslavement to creditors. To enjoy this freedom, we must learn to recognize the dangers of deceitful advertising and to avoid the dangers of easy credit. Failure to do either almost always leads us into the dangers of undisciplined budgeting.

"Know well the condition of your flocks, and pay attention to your herds" (Prov. 27:23). What does that mean to us today? It means that we should be fully aware of what's going on in our finances. We should know our net worth, our monthly expenses, and our spending limits. Do you know how much money you spent last month? Do you know how much you can spend this month? Would you be able to pay an unexpected medical bill next month?

In our home, we use a detailed monthly budget system with carefully defined spending limits, and when I taught this series in our church, I strongly encouraged every church family to adopt a similar plan. Most families need a budget for one of two reasons. Either they are living beyond their income and they need the budget to help them limit unnecesary spending so they can pay their bills and learn to live within their means. Or, their income signficantly exceeds their actual living expenses, and they need the budget to help them resist the temptation to make purchases which, though easily affordable, are simply not God-honoring. In other words, their budget helps them limit their spending so they can use their excess money in ways that would honor God or further His kingdom, rather than for the fulfillment of their own desires.

My father used to say that if a man earns $12,000 a year, he will spend $12,000 a year; if he earns $120,000 a year, he will spend $120,000 a year. When left to our own undisciplined ways, most of us end up proving that statement to be true. The more we earn, the more we spend, so we never establish a reserve of excess funds which can be used in God-directed ways.

Recently, Lynne and I were able to give a friend $1,000. That was exciting for us because it was the first time in our married life that we had enough excess money to be able to help someone else in a substantial way. We now enjoy being able to lay a certain portion of money before the Lord and say, "Here it is, Lord. Please bring someone across our path who needs our excess." I think it pleases God to see us budgeting with discipline and frugality so that we can establish a reserve fund that can be used to meet another family's needs, either through an interest-free loan or an outright gift—

whichever the Lord prompts us to do.

I believe so firmly in budgeting that I enlisted Bruce Saarela, a member of our church board, to present to our entire congregation a detailed, organized method for establishing a personal family budget. Bruce not only gave us the specific tools necessary for making wise financial decisions, but he also opened the doors of communication so that adults in our church could begin to talk with one another about their financial needs and frustrations. The result is that many of our church families are now handling their personal finances in a more disciplined, godly way than they ever have before, and they're enjoying greater freedom from financial bondage and tension.

That we manage our money well is extremely important to God. It tells Him that we are committed to being good stewards of our gifts and responsibilities, be they great or small.

Let us close this chapter with one more thought from God's Word. "If therefore you have not been faithful in the use of unrighteous mammon [money], who will entrust the true riches to you?" (Luke 16:11) What, in God's eyes, are true riches? People! There's nothing more precious to Him than people, the crown of His creation, and there's no greater responsibility that He offers to any of us than the spiritual nurturing of other people. In this verse, Jesus establishes a direct correlation between fiscal responsibilities and people-centered responsibilities.

Many Christians are concerned about their lack of impact in other people's lives. Might it not be that they have failed to handle responsibly the money God has entrusted to them? How then can He entrust to them the true riches, people?

I hope and pray that you will take action on what you have just read. As you do, you can trust that God will begin to entrust more people to your care. He who is faithful with little will be made faithful in much (Luke 16:10).

Eight

The Christian Investor

The Christian worker who labors diligently in the marketplace will inevitably be rewarded for his diligence with increased wages. If he then uses these wages wisely by decreasing the amount of frivolous spending, making necessary purchases thoughtfully, and budgeting carefully, he will begin to enjoy the freedom of having surplus finances. This happy situation is not, however, the end of the financial story. The next step is to wisely invest these surplus funds so that they can earn a God-glorifying return through both *temporal* investments and *eternal* investments.

Making wise temporal investments demands that we become educated in money market funds, stocks and bonds, CDs, T-bills, etc. Professional investment counselors can assist us in this area by providing the necessary information and giving us experienced counsel. Because I am not one of these professionals, and certainly do not consider myself competent to address the subject in an in-depth manner, I will not attempt to do so. I do, however, want to take a serious look at what the Bible says about *eternal* investments.

How to Be "Rich Toward God"
In many places throughout Scripture God warns us not to become so caught up in temporal financial concerns that we forget to be "rich toward God" (Luke 12:21). He calls those of us who know His Son as Lord and Saviour to make regular and generous monetary investments in the work of His kingdom, both as a demonstration of our willingness to be obedient to Him, and as a practical, tangible

means of helping to expand the influence of His church throughout the community and the world.

One of the most colorful passages that instructs believers to give generously to the Lord's work is 2 Corinthians 9:6-8, 10-11. The Apostle Paul, speaking under the inspiration of the Holy Spirit, says, "Now this I say, he who sows sparingly shall also reap sparingly; and he who sows bountifully shall also reap bountifully. Let each one do just as he has purposed in his heart; not grudgingly or under compulsion; for God loves a cheerful giver. And God is able to make all grace abound to you, that always having all sufficiency in everything, you may have an abundance for every good deed. . . . Now He who supplies seed to the sower and bread for food, will supply and multiply your seed for sowing and increase the harvest of your righteousness; you will be enriched in everything for all liberality, which through us is producing thanksgiving to God."

Though many of us tend to think that bankers, stockbrokers, investment counselors, trust officers, and similar professionals are the only experts in investment, Paul recognized that probably no one knows more about the principle of investment than farmers. For thousands of years farmers have anxiously awaited springtime, eager to plow the fields and prepare the soil, knowing that soon they would make the most daring and crucial investment of their year. Then, scraping together every cent they could find, they bought as much seed as they possibly could, understanding full well the principle given in 2 Corinthians 9:6. If they bought a minimal amount of seed and planted sparsely, they could expect nothing more than a light harvest, a meager return; but if they made a heavy investment and planted generously, they could expect to enjoy the fruits of a bountiful harvest.

Every farmer hopes for a bumper crop. He relishes the thought of an abundant harvest. So what does he do? He applies the principle of investment. No seed; no harvest. Generous seed; generous harvest.

In addition to the principle of investment, the farmer understands the principl of increase. He knows not only that he must sow to reap, but also that he will reap more than he sows. Through a miracle of nature under the direction of God, a seed that is planted in the ground returns in multiplied form. A farmer today who plants 2 bushels of wheat can anticipate a harvest of 67 bushels. When 3 bushels of oats are planted, God's miraculous principle of increase produces 79 bushels. One - third of a bushel of corn, planted and harvested, will bring a yield of 120 bushels. Do you see now why farmers are experts in investment and increase?

A friend of mine has a small, backyard garden which he tends lovingly and meticulously. Each time I visit him he graciously offers me grocery bags filled with the surplus of his labors, surplus enough to feed my family, as well as his own, for the entire summer. Here again we see the principle of increase. A few handfuls of seed, planted and carefully nurtured, yield a return bountiful enough to feed two families for several months.

Investment, increase, and finally, interval. The farmer knows that he must sow in order to reap and that he will reap more than he sows, but he also knows that he must wait patiently during the period of interval. If he plants in April, he will harvest in September. If he plants in June, he will harvest in October. He cannot alter that pattern. He cannot escape the period of waiting. So he learns to be patient, trusting that the planting will indeed result in a harvest. He doesn't become doubtful when the seed fails to mature overnight. He understands the principle of interval and realizes that it is as essential to the harvest as is the planting.

What the Principles Teach Us

But what does this passage say to us 20th-century Christians whose labor takes place not in the fields of an agricultural society but in the workplaces of a technical world, and whose concern is not to understand God's principles as they relate to the harvest of grains and vegetables, but as they relate to our personal finances? What can we learn from these principles?

We can learn first that if we want God's full blessing on our personal finances, we must learn to *sow*. We must learn to invest a portion of what we have earned by giving it back to the Lord, thereby giving Him the opportunity to bring about a supernatural increase. In short, we need to learn to *give*.

Whenever the subject of giving is raised, four questions are inevitably asked: Who should give? When should we give? Where should we give? How much should we give? Paul answered these questions for the Corinthians: "Now concerning the collection for the saints, as I directed the churches of Galatia, so do you also. On the first day of every week let each one of you put aside and save, as he may prosper, that no collections be made when I come" (1 Cor. 16:1-2). Who should give? "Each one of you," says Paul. This means that every person who is a part of the family of God has been called by God to be a part of the giving, supporting unit that works together to facilitate the spread of the Gospel message and the ministry of the church. Paul didn't give his directive only to the wealthy, the prosperous, those who had a special gift of giving. He urged every single person who was a part of the church at Corinth to give to the work of the Lord.

In the body of Christ there is little room for exceptions. We all are sinners. We all must bow down before Christ and by grace receive Him as Saviour and Lord. We all anticipate a home in heaven for eternity. We all have been given spiritual gifts that we must develop and use for God's glory. And we all are called to give of our financial resources for the ministry of the church. Churches that are supported by isolated handfuls of faithful "givers" are evidence of the lack of understanding many Christians have of their responsibility, and of God's command, to give.

The first question is "Who should give?" The second question is "When should we give?" Can we give once a year? Can we give now and then, whenever "the Spirit moves?" Can we give only when we have excess cash? Again in 1 Corinthians 16:2 we read, *"On the first day of every week* let each one of you put aside" (italics added). The important issue here is not what day we consider to be the first day of the week, or on what day we write out our check, or whether we put it in the offering plate or send it in the mail. The issue is consistency. We are called to give on a regular basis according to the established weekly cycle. As we gather each week to study, to grow, and to worship, we should come prepared also to join together in giving. Not only does this enable the ministry of the church to continue undaunted by financial insecurity, but it allows us to regularly show our appreciation for God and the work He has done in our lives. God's love is consistent each week. He assists us in our labors throughout the workdays of every week. Is it any surprise then that He asks us to give to His work in the same manner?

The third question is "Where should we give?" Should we give to TV ministries? To charitable organizations? To needy individuals? To everyone who asks for help? In the Bible we read, "Bring the whole tithe into the storehouse, so that there may be food in My house" (Mal. 3:10). The storehouse at that time was the gathering place for the goods of the community and contained the treasury box for a particular congregation. It was there that the children of God were to bring their tithes.

In Mark 12:41 we read about the central temple treasury where those who worshiped in the temple brought their gifts each week, and in Paul's epistles there are numerous references to collections being made by the various local church bodies. Scripture appears, then, to indicate that our primary financial allegiance should be to our local churches.

It may be helpful to ask these questions when determining where to give. Where do I receive my primary spiritual feeding? Where do my children receive nurturing, care, and teaching? Where would I turn for help in a crisis? Where do I use my spiritual gifts? The answer to these questions should be, and usually is, the local church.

A man once told me that he regularly gave all the money that he felt should go to God's work to a relative who was crippled, unable to work, and desperately in need of support. He felt that by so doing he was fulfilling his obligation to the Lord's work. While I commended him for his concern for his relative, I could not help but add to my response a word of caution. If everyone decided to give wherever he wanted to, with no thought of his responsibility to the local body, the overall ministry of the church would be hindered, and perhaps even prohibited. Lynne and I have long felt compelled to contribute to other ministries outside our own church, but we have done so only after prayerfully determining what God would have us give to our church.

How Much to Give?

"Who? When? And where? But now comes the big question: "How much should we give?" Some preach that if we don't give everything, we haven't given enough, and they burden us with demands that can never be met. Because we know we can't "give everything," that such demands are impossible to fulfill, we defensively give our $5 (or whatever offering is "painless" for us), and consider ourselves "paid-up." We've done our part!

But we certainly haven't done it according to biblical standards. The Bible speaks of two distinct categories of giving, the first being the tithe and the second being the freewill gift. The tithe, which means one-tenth, is first mentioned in Genesis 14:20 where Abraham gave a tithe of all that he had to the high priest Melchizedek. The word reappears throughout the Old Testament, but one of the key passages in which it appears is Malachi 3:8-10: "'Will a man rob God? Yet you are robbing Me! But you say, "How have we robbed Thee?" In tithes and offerings. You are cursed with a curse, for you are robbing Me, the whole nation of you! Bring the whole tithe into the storehouse, so that there may be food in My house, and test Me now in this,' says the Lord of hosts, 'if I will not open for you the windows of heaven, and pour out for you a blessing until it overflows.'"

God promised to pour out on the nation of Israel a blessing that would be beyond their wildest expectations, but on what was it contingent? The whole tithe. Many people feel uncomfortable with the teaching on tithing because its legalistic ring conflicts with their idea of "freedom in Christ." To them the tithe sounds too much like paying weekly dues. But is there not a far deeper issue at stake here than personal preferences? What about the issue of obedience? Have they forgotten that all we have as believers is God's and He has every right to make a claim on it? Many believe and teach that the tithe was strictly for Israel and doesn't apply to God's people today. I am not in that number: my study of God's Word persuades me to believe that Christians should tithe.

God has given us the ability to work and receive financial compensation for that work. He has also made His wisdom available to us as we decide how to spend our wages. He asks that we give back to Him one-tenth of what we have earned, as a means of proving that we have indeed given Him control of our lives, that we consider Him our Lord and the owner of all that we have. He has every right to ask for 20 percent, for 40 percent, for 90 percent! But He only asks His people for the tithe. Is obedience to that standard too much to ask?

In Matthew 23:23 Jesus said, "Woe to you scribes and Pharisees, hypocrites! For you tithe mint and dill and cummin, and have neglected the weightier provision of the law: justice and mercy and faithfulness; but these are the things you should have done without neglecting the others." To claim that our tithe is the ultimate and total fulfillment of obedience to God is to make a false claim, for, as

Jesus said, justice and mercy and faithfulness are surely "weightier" concerns. But to claim that Jesus' words in this passage minimize the significance of the tithe is equally false. "These are the things you should have done *without* neglecting the others [the tithes]." Jesus tells us to be faithful in all of these things. As justice and mercy and faithfulness are matters of obedience, so is the tithe.

Robbing God

Malachi 3 says plainly that if we are not tithing we are robbing God of what is rightfully His, and by doing that we remove ourselves from the umbrella of His fullest blessing. We may be obedient with respect to morality, relationships, and family responsibilities, and we may be faithful and diligent workers in the marketplace, but if we fail to be obedient to God with respect to our giving, we will limit the scope of God's blessing on our lives.

Some people ask whether they should tithe their net income or their gross income, and what they should do about monetary gifts, royalties, bonuses, etc. Personally, I feel that we should tithe every form of income we receive in its full gross amount, remembering that we will be amply rewarded. If we sow sparingly we will reap sparingly, but if we sow bountifully we will reap bountifully. We have nothing to lose by being generous with the Lord!

The second type of giving is freewill giving. From time to time we are given opportunities to give that go beyond the required tithe and allow us to show our gratitude to God, and our concern for the needs of other people. This may mean sponsoring a needy child through an organization such as World Vision, as Lynne and I have chosen to do, or giving to other service-oriented Christian organizations. It may mean giving a special gift to our local church, in addition to our regular tithe. It may even mean supporting individual missionaries or friends and relatives with unique needs. The opportunities are endless! Such giving is to be done in answer to the quiet prompting of the Holy Spirit, and only as it can be done with a cheerful heart.

The Apostle Paul reminds us that "God loves a cheerful giver" (2 Cor. 9:7).

There is a sense to which we are called to give the tithe whether we "feel like it" or not, by simply making a decision of the will to respond obediently to God's commands. Many times I don't feel like loving my enemies; in fact, I may feel like attacking and destroying them. However in obedience to God I have to treat them as Christ treated me, with grace and forgiveness. The same is true with the tithe. We need to do it because God demands it. The freewill gift is different, however, in the sense that it is not a response to an absolute rule. It is, rather, the response of a loving, thankful heart that has known the blessing of the Lord and is internally compelled to share that blessing with others. It is less a matter of obedience than a matter of overflowing love.

So, then, who should give? Each one who claims Jesus as Saviour and Lord. When should we give? On a regular weekly basis. Where should we give? First to the local church, then as God directs. How much should we give? At least the tithe. If we want to reap, we have to sow, by obediently giving a portion of our earnings back to the Lord. That is the principle of investment.

But now, what of the principle of increase? Seldom in Scripture does God challenge us to test Him, but so eager is He to abundantly bless us through the principle of increase that He asks us to test His word. "Do what I ask of you," He says. "Then watch and see what I will do for you. I will pour out on you a blessing that will more than meet your every need! Try me, and see!" (See Mal. 3:10.) He's asking us to test the principle of increase.

Jesus said, "Give, and it will be given to you; good measure, pressed down, shaken together, running over, they will pour into your lap" (Luke 6:38). When we give God the tithe, He brings supernatural power to bear on that gift and returns it to us in multiplied form, just as He gives the farmer the multiplied bushels of corn, wheat, and oats.

Never in my life have I heard of a sincere and obedient Christian (one who has acknowledged Christ as Lord and wholeheartedly attempts to live a pure and godly life) who has felt that God has been unfaithful in fulfilling His promise in regard to the tithe. I have occasionally heard that complaint from some insincere and disobedient Christians, men and women who have been inconsistent givers, or who have been living in deliberate impurity in other areas of their lives, thereby disqualifying themselves from receiving God's full blessings. Never, however, have I known a man or woman who has sought to live purely before the Lord and has given faithfully in obedience to God's Word who has not received God's reward in multiplied form.

How God Has Blessed Lynne and Me

Though I hesitate to use Lynne and myself as an illustration of this principle, I do so because I earnestly believe that God has proven Himself to be faithful in such a dramatic way in our lives. When we first began ministering at Willow Creek Community Church, we received no form of income from the church; so I worked many nights at the South Water Street Market in Chicago, buying produce for our family produce company in Michigan. At the same time Lynne taught private music lessons at a local high school. On a good week our income averaged between $50 and $60, hardly enough to support a young couple struggling to establish a home and family. Yet, we dared not neglect our giving. Though our meager tithe did little to advance the kingdom of God, it was one way for us to display our willingness to obey God, thereby freeing Him to give us His full blessing.

God honored our giving, and soon the church was able to begin supporting us, first in a small way, but now to the point where I believe I am paid far more than I'm worth, and Lynne and I are able to enjoy not only the bountiful gifts that God has given us, but also the freedom to give further to God's work. When I read 2 Corinthians 9:11 it seems to say, "Lynne and Bill have been enriched in everything. They have cause for all liberality. And they are so thankful to God!" Our part was simply to obey God in giving. His part was to bring the increase, "in good measure, pressed down, shaken together, running over, pouring into our lap." How faithful He has been to us!

The principle of increase does not mean that every faithful giver will become wealthy by earthly standards. It does mean, however, that our every need will be more than adequately met through the gracious blessing of a kind and loving Father.

Wait Patiently

The principle of investment is obvious, practical, and easy to understand. The principle of increase is equally easy to understand and a tremendous source of encouragement for the sincere giver. But the principle of interval is often misunderstood and frequently the source of frustration and doubts. Though the farmer understands and accepts the fact that he cannot expect the harvest to take place immediately after planting, many Christians fail to understand that they too may have to wait patiently during the time of interval, trusting that the harvest will come in due season. I've received many calls from people who have said, "I began tithing two weeks ago and I haven't yet seen the harvest. What's wrong with God?" My only answer is, "If the farmer planted corn two weeks ago, would he be enjoying corn-on-the-cob tonight?"

Usually these people call me several months later and say, "I feel so foolish for expecting the harvest to come overnight. God has indeed been faithful. As we have continued to give with joyful hearts in obedience to His Word, He has faithfully brought the increase."

"Oh, I understand," some of you may be thinking. "I give so I can get. This whole tithing issue is nothing more than a practical money-making venture for me." No. We give in obedience to God's Word. However, after we obey, and on the basis of that act of obedience, we can expect God to do what He has promised to do, "to enrich us in everything *for all liberality*." We don't give so that we can get. We give so that we can give again even more liberally. The Apostle Paul tells us that God gives us "sufficiency in everything" so that we can have "an abundance for every good deed" (2 Cor. 9:8). The giving process becomes an upward spiral. The more we give, the more we experience God's blessings in every area of our lives, and the more we desire and are able to give even more to "every good deed" as a means of serving the kingdom of God.

As Christians, we believe in God for our salvation through Christ; we believe in God for our eternal destination in heaven; and we believe that God will provide the indwelling Holy Spirit to work in our lives. Can we not also trust Him to be faithful in giving an abundant return on our eternal investments? What glory would come to Him and how the work of the kingdom would prosper if every Christian became obedient in tithing to his or her local church. The result would be awesome. First, God's blessing would fall on the individual sower, the Christian giver. Second, God's blessing would fall on the local communities of believers and its influence could expand throughout the community and the world. And third, and most importantly, God would be glorified by their obedience.

God wants us to labor diligently in the marketplace. He wants us to spend carefully as Christian consumers. And He wants us to give generously as obedient children of God. If we work and spend and give according to the principles of God's Word, we will be enriched in all things!

Nine

You and Self-Confidence

Imagine two women sitting in the personnel office of a large company waiting to interview for the same job. They have each been out of the job market for nearly 20 years, having worked hard as homemakers, wives, and mothers. Now, as their youngest children enter high school, they decide that it's time to reevaluate their abilities, their needs, and their priorities. It's time for a change.

The first woman enters the office for the interview. Even as she moves across the room, her feelings of fear and insecurity begin to surface. "What am I doing here?" she asks herself. "What do I have to offer?" In the security of her own kitchen she felt she was ready for a change. Now she's not so sure.

The interviewer asks his first question. "What makes you think you are qualified for this position?" Though he asks the question kindly and offers a pleasant smile, the gentle encouragement is no match for the overwhelming despair that descends on her thoughts. Fighting back the tears, she mumbles, "Oh, I don't know. I was just bored. I'm only a housewife." She exits as soon as possible, ravaged by self-doubt and self-pity.

The second woman then enters the room. She holds her head high, walks briskly, and chooses the chair directly opposite the personnel manager. Looking him straight in the eyes, she listens intently to his first question. "What makes you think you are qualified to handle this position?"

She smiles, and begins. "I believe I am uniquely qualified for this

97

job. I have been a devoted wife, mother, and homemaker for the past 20 years. I have personally tutored four children through grade school and junior high, become an expert on new math, new English, and new morality. I have also served as their resident guidance counselor, thoughtfully advising them and their friends on every subject from dating to college selection. In addition to being a dedicated mother, I have also proven myself to be a capable administrator, efficiently organizing and scheduling the activities of a busy household. During the past 20 years I have served my family as a purchasing agent, a real estate broker (I have bought and sold three homes and each time made wise decisions that resulted in profitable transactions), a financier, and a gourmet cook. I have kept my family intact through 20 years of joys and sorrows, laughter and tears. And that takes a level of commitment, sacrifice, and hard work that can't be questioned. I know I can handle this job!"

These two women share similar backgrounds in terms of educational experience and socioeconomic environment, yet when it comes to their attitude concerning their own abilities, the similarity abruptly ends. Why?

Nurturing Self-Confidence

Early in my ministry I realized the importance of self-esteem. I knew that if men and women were to reach their highest potential as godly husbands, wives, parents, employees, employers, and ultimately as faithful servants of the Lord, they had to understand their intrinsic value as creations of a loving God. Only then would they be free to respond to Him with joyful hearts, use their spiritual gifts in the body of Christ, and accept the other challenges that He would bring their way. Consequently, it was tremendously exciting for me to see people developing a healthy self-esteem as I and other members of our church staff began to teach about the love of God and the value of man. We knew that this was the key to their personal satisfaction and productivity.

There was along the way, however, a certain amount of frustration as we saw some individuals who continued to be burdened with fear and insecurity despite their growing knowledge of God and His love for them. Though they intellectually acknowledged their value to God, they remained dissatisfied with who they were, fearful of the future, uncomfortable with their abilities, and unwilling to accept new challenges. Like the first woman described in the illustration, they lacked self-confidence.

What I didn't realize at that time is that there is a significant difference between having a realistic appraisal of our *ultimate worth,* which is the basis of self-esteem, and having an accurate evaluation of our *actual abilities,* which is the basis of self-confidence.

The process of evaluating our abilities begins in childhood. Because a child is born in the image of God, he has at least a trace of God's creative personality. He is dynamic, growing ever new. He has an inborn desire to learn and experiment. He wants to determine his abilities and express them. He wants to find out what that little body and mind of his can do, and he wants to do it!

That's why it's so important that parents provide a secure and loving environment in which their children feel free to experiment with newfound abilities and try out new ideas, knowing that an occasional failure will not jeopardize their parents' unconditional love for them. The quality of a child's performance (whether he's learning to ride a new bicycle or spell his name) is not all that important. What is important is that he has the freedom to learn and grow and experiment.

In addition to an environment that provides the *freedom* to experiment, parents must also provide their children with ample *opportunity* to experiment, to test a variety of abilities, both physical and mental. The only way to determine our strengths and weaknesses is to test our abilities in different situations. Many people have missed out on tremendous satisfaction and enjoyment simply because they never had the opportunity to test that one skill that would have given them a glimpse of their true potential. Sports, crafts, books, games, trips, pets, classes, music lessons, relationships—these are all avenues through which we test our arms, our legs, our minds, our interests, our aptitudes. Experimentation is the *only* way to test and prove our abilities.

Along with the freedom and opportunity to experiment, parents must also provide their children with healthy amounts of affirmation. Children must be praised for their skills and achievements. "That's a great idea! What a beautiful picture! How did you do that trick? Can you do it again?" Just like us, they need to know that what they do is good, and they can only know that if it is affirmed by someone else.

It's important to look at our roots as related to self-confidence. Did we grow up in an environment that supplied freedom, opportunity, and affirmation? Were we able to test our abilities and determine our strengths? Did we have a series of success experiences on which to build?

I am so thankful for the heritage which I had, one that provided a perfect setting for building self-confidence. My father threw challenge after challenge my way and helped me to meet those challenges in such a way that I had frequent success experiences. But along with the success experiences, he gave me something equally important—the freedom to fail. In fact, sometimes I think he almost welcomed an occasional failure because it afforded him the opportunity to teach me the proper way to view failure.

Most people attribute their failures to their lack of ability. Each time they fail, they conclude that they're just not smart enough, or not strong enough, or not creative enough, etc. As this pattern becomes entrenched in their thinking, they fall victim to self-doubt and begin to distrust their abilities more and more.

What is needed to break this self-defeating pattern of thinking is a clearer understanding of failure and a means of turning failures into positive growing experiences.

Experience Needed

Not long ago I watched an exciting football game between the Chicago Bears and the Dallas Cowboys. Since the Cowboys had thoroughly humiliated the Bears in a previous game, I was anxious to see the Bears get their revenge.

With two minutes left in the fourth quarter the Bears were ahead, but it was obvious that Dallas wasn't going to give up without a fight. Down the field marched the Cowboy quarterback, passing at will through the seams in the Bear defense. When he got to the 20-yard line, the camera picked him up on an end-zone shot. There he stood, cool and confident, looking the Bear defensemen straight in the eyes.

The ball was snapped. As the QB stepped back into the pocket, the Dallas tight end made an unbelievable move on the line of scrimmage and ran a totally unexpected pattern. At the same time, the QB threw a perfect pass. Doug Plank, the Bear free safety assigned to cover the receiver, stretched out horizontally in the air in a valiant attempt to break up the pass, but the ball passed just inches from his fingertips. Dallas made the reception that set up the touchdown that gave them the game.

Two days later I attended a press luncheon and listened as a reporter asked Doug Plank what went wrong on that play. As soon as I heard the question I thought, "Come on, why give the guy a hard time? He probably feels terrible about that play." I expected Doug to say that he just wasn't fast enough, that his lateral movement wasn't all it should be, or that he hadn't conditioned properly for the game, or to give some other expression of self-doubt.

Instead, Doug said, "Sir, let me tell you exactly what happened on that play. I was ready to cover my man, I knew the QB was going to pass to him, and I was geared up for the play. But quite frankly, what happened right after the ball was snapped took me by complete surprise. The Dallas tight end pulled one of the most creative moves off the line of scrimmage that I have ever seen. I honestly thought that he was out of the play. I didn't think there was the remotest chance that he could receive the pass. But all of a sudden I realized that he was running a perfectly planned pattern and he was right in position. At that point I did my best to break up the pass, but I was too late.

"I know that some people might accuse me of lacking ability, but it's not true; I'm fast enough and I move well. The truth is that I had simply never seen a move like that before in my life. It was totally new to me. I'll tell you something, though, sir. If anybody ever tries that move on me again, I'll be on him like a shirt! I'll never miss a play like that again!"

Doug Plank knew why he had missed that play. He lacked the necessary experience. He just hadn't seen a play like that before. Many people attribute their defeats to a lack of ability, when in reality all they lack is experience.

Frequently, as workers in the marketplace, we are plunged into new experiences for which we feel inadequately prepared. Many of us become discouraged when we face the demands of the new job or responsibility, or when we make mistakes. The key to overcoming these feelings of self-doubt is to remind ourselves that in order to succeed in anything, we need to gain the necessary experience, and gaining experience almost always involves making mistakes. The important thing is to learn from these mistakes and apply the lessons learned to tomorrow's challenges.

Statistics have shown that more college students withdraw from school during their freshman year, immediately after first semester grades are released, than at any other time during college. When I was a youth minister, I talked with many of these kids who claimed that they just didn't have the intelligence needed to succeed in college. In the vast majority of these cases, I think the real problem was that they just hadn't adjusted to college life. They hadn't learned to study properly, to prepare assignments, and to take tests. They didn't lack intelligence; they simply lacked experience. Had they stayed long enough to develop a clearer understanding of the expectations and to perfect their study skills, they probably could have succeeded.

Most unsuccessful small businesses also collapse during the first year of business. For example, in one case as business began to fail, the proprietor gave in to self-doubt and concluded that he simply didn't have the ability to manage his own business. Soon he quit. The truth may be that he simply lacked experience in the necessary aspects of running a business that could have only been gained by "doing." Provided that he was offering a sound product or service for which there was a reasonable market, he probably could have succeeded had he persevered long enough to develop the necessary skills.

Too Much?

If the average ninth-grader were suddenly whisked into graduate school, would his failure to make the grade indicate a lack of ability? Certainly not. It would be the expected result of giving him an unreasonable challenge. When we fail we must first ask ourselves if we lack the necessary experience. Then we should ask ourselves if we have taken on an unrealistic challenge.

I remember reading the story of an excellent high school pitcher who was drafted by the Texas Rangers. This young man had extraordinary ability, but he was no match for the more experienced professionals. After just three innings in his first pro game, this outstanding young athlete became so discouraged that he left the game and never played baseball again. Had he risen through the normal ranks of the minor league teams, he might be a great ball player today. Unfortunately, he was defeated by the overwhelming frustration of an unrealistic challenge.

One of the most serious responsibilities of parenting is to accurately assess our children's abilities so we can offer opportunities that will challenge, but not unnecessarily frustrate them. This is also one of the great challenges of management.

One of my most important responsibilities as the senior pastor at our church is to make sure that each of our 22 staff members is in a position that is challenging, but not overly demanding, and that it makes the best use of his or her unique abilities. In order to do this, I make every effort to keep lines of communication open at all times, so that staff members feel free to discuss minor frustrations which, if ignored, could lead to more serious problems. I also meet formally once a week with all staff members who report directly to me, so that we can mutually evaluate the quality of work and the level of personal fulfillment that is associated with his or her job.

If there are any significant problems in either area, we try to answer these questions. Is his or her job description too broad? Do his responsibilities lie outside his range of natural abilities or spiritual gifts? Do they require the use of skills that he has not yet acquired? Are there other responsibilities that he feels more competent to handle? Is he unmotivated because he has to spend a majority of his time doing tasks that he doesn't enjoy? Every job has certain elements that are not enjoyable but ideally these elements should not take up a majority of our work time.

Frequently we have found that staff members felt frustrated and overworked simply because they were doing the wrong jobs. They were expected to handle responsibilities that did not take into consideration their unique skills and spiritual gifts, and which consequently presented them with unrealistic challenges. In other cases, they felt overworked because, in fact, they were. Their job descriptions were too inclusive. In both cases, a slight rearrangement of responsibilities was all that was needed to solve the problems.

A businessman recently told me that he was prepared to fire a certain employee because he appeared to be incompetent and uncommitted, but he wanted to make one last effort to determine if there were any unknown factors that might be contributing to the problem. In talking with the employee, he learned that after a recent department reorganization, this man had been given several responsibilities that should have been given to another worker. It was apparent at that point that the man did not lack ability; he was simply burdened with an overwhelming workload.

Before we let failure defeat us, we must ask ourselves some honest questions. Have we taken on too much work or responsibility? Are we in the wrong position? Are we trying to use abilities we don't have? In short, are we grappling with an unrealistic challenge?

A Poor Teacher

In response to failure we should ask ourselves three questions: "Do I lack experience?" "Have I taken on an unrealistic challenge?" and now, "Did I receive inadequate training?"

Shortly after Lynne and I were married, we took a camping trip to Northern Michigan. We took with us two small motorbikes so that we could enjoy the lovely trails that wound through the acres and acres of beautiful forest land surrounding the campsite. Lynne had never driven a motorcycle, but I was confident that she could do it. "After all," I thought. "It's easy for me. Why should she have any trouble?"

On the second day of our trip, I took the bike off the trailer, started it up, and told her to hop on. I explained how to operate the clutch, and showed her where the throttle and brake were located. That was it. As far as I was concerned she was ready to take off!

But as soon as she turned the throttle, I knew she was in trouble. The bike was out of control. It started going faster and faster, round and round the campsite. Mothers grabbed their kids! I hid behind a tree! The whirlwind blitz came to an end only when she hit a garbage can and crashed into a pile of dead leaves. I couldn't believe it. How could she be so uncoordinated? Why didn't she catch on?

Needless to say, we put the bike away and spent the rest of the vacation riding double on my bike.

Several years later, Lynne again decided to test her skills on a motorcycle. This time she was in Michigan visiting her parents and was under the instruction of her father, a patient and thorough teacher. He used a small trail bike and explained in detail exactly how the bike operated and what she had to do to handle it properly. He told her when to shift, how to use the clutch and throttle together to execute smooth starts, how to lean into turns, etc.

After two or three hours, she had become proficient on that bike, so she moved up to a bigger one. This time her dad sat behind her as they rode along the country roads. He told her what to look for in terms of rough road conditions and drilled her on the importance of defensive driving.

The next day she moved up to an even bigger bike, and by the time she returned home, she had made her solo run on a Harley Davidson Sportster, a bike many times larger than the little trail bike she had crashed into a garbage can just a few years earlier!

Was it ability she had lacked on that first attempt? Obviously not! She'd just lacked the proper training. She'd lacked a good teacher.

The marketplace is famous for its failure to provide adequate on-the-job training, though fortunately, many of the more progressive companies are beginning to develop effective training programs for their employees. If such programs are available to you, take every advantage of them. If they're not available, take the initiative to seek help from more experienced or more knowledgeable people in your department, or contact a friend or acquaintance in a similar capacity in another department or company. Make use of outside resource materials, such as business magazines, periodicals, and trade publications, and see if local universities or community colleges offer classes that might be helpful to you.

Don't let inadequate training stop you. Take the initiative to get the training you need!

Building Self-confidence

The first woman described in the illustration which opened this chapter is a perfect example of what I call the "withering worm." Compliant, fearful, and easily intimidated, the withering worm fears competition because he doubts his abilities, avoids confrontation become he doubts his character, and is unable to express firm conviction because he doubts his beliefs. His basic problem is that he lacks self-confidence.

The opposite behavior is exhibited by the "obnoxious egotist," who also lacks self-confidence, but compensates for it by being boastful and arrogant. He's a frequent name-dropper, enjoys engaging in self-exalting conversations, and rarely admits to being wrong. He craves power and is happy only when he successfully elevates himself into a position above others.

Most of us would have to admit that occasionally we exhibit

varying degrees of these negative behavioral patterns. Because we experience feelings of self-doubt which we don't know how to handle constructively, we slip into the self-pitying pose of the withering worm, or we adopt the ugly mask of the obnoxious egotist.

Certainly we can do ourselves (and others!) a favor if we will acknowledge these feelings of self-doubt and take some practical steps toward developing self-confidence, first by examining our failures in light of the guidelines just discussed, and then by accepting the positive challenges presented in the remainder of this chapter.

Specify Abilities

Imagine how you would feel if your little son or daughter came to you and said, "Mommy, Daddy, when you made me you really goofed. I have no brains, no character, and no personality. I can't do anything right. You made a big mistake when you made me!" I would be heartbroken if one of my children said that to me, because I know it's not true.

Yet how many times have I been tempted to say that to God? "You blew it when You made me! I'm a failure! I can't do anything right!" How different those words are from the words that David wrote in Psalm 139:14-15: "I will give thanks to Thee, for I am fearfully and wonderfully made; wonderful are Thy works, and my soul knows it very well. My frame was not hidden from Thee, when I was made in secret, and skillfully wrought in the depths of the earth." David didn't have a "puffed up" view of himself. A quick reading through the Psalms assures us that David lived in the utmost humility before the Lord. He had, however, a realistic view of himself. He knew that he was a creation of God, and as such was "wonderfully made" and "skillfully wrought." He knew that he was made in the image of God, and even though that image was stained by imperfection, it still spoke of the wonder of God.

We are told in Scripture not to think more highly of ourselves than we should, but "to think so as to have sound judgment" (Rom. 12:3). What does it mean to see ourselves with sound judgment? It means, simply, to see ourselves as truthfully and accurately as possible. We are not to regard ourselves too highly, as Paul warns, but neither are we to adopt a "low" view of ourselves, as many people tend to do. They refuse to acknowledge (or perhaps are unable to see) the strengths, abilities, and gifts that God has given them. They view themselves through overly critical, rather than honest, eyes.

The first step in learning to view ourselves honestly is to specify our abilities. We do this by examining the success experiences we have had in the past and pinpointing the specific abilities that we used to succeed in those situations. What were the specific physical, intellectual, creative, or relational abilities we used to succeeed? Did we show a special ability to work well with other people in a team situation? Did we exhibit leadership abilities? Are we good at working with our hands? Can we easily come up with new and creative ideas? Do we find it easy to memorize? Are we good at sports? Do we have administrative abilities? Do we have a special gift of compassion, or patience, or encouragement? Are we able to spend long hours alone working on projects that demand intense concentration?

The answers to questions like these can help us develop a profile of our abilities that is essential to the building of self-confidence.

Another way to specify our abilities is to look at ourselves through the eyes of a close observer. Other people often have a clearer, and certainly more objective view of our abilities than we have. I'm sure this principle is operative in the biannual evaluations which I have with the church staff. Frequently, I am able to point out to them the specific abilities (or spiritual gifts) that allow them to be successful and satisfied in one area of their work, while they may be frustrated in another area. Likewise, it is often through the eyes of my wife, my close friends, or the elders under whose authority I work that I most clearly see my own abilities (as well as my own liabilities).

Since the key to specifying our abilities is experimentation, those of us who had the opportunity to experiment freely have probably already learned to specify our abilities. For those who did not have that opportunity, *today is the day to begin!* The only way to become acquainted with our abilities is to try new things. Each time we do that, we have the opportunity to ask ourselves questions that will help us learn the truth about our abilities. Undoubtedly there will be times when our experimenting only teaches us what we can't do or what we don't enjoy, but that too is a necessary part of the process. Only by eliminating possibilities can we determine where to focus our energies.

Stretch Your Abilities

I have fantasized telling my Sunday morning congregation that when they go to the parking lot after the service they will find their cars replaced by helicopters. In each helicopter is an instructor prepared to teach the owner of each "vanished" car how to fly and land in his own backyard. Not until he arrives home will he have his car returned.

If I could really convince the entire congregation that I had done this, I think I would see people reacting in one of two distinctly different ways. The people in the first group would probably break out in hives. Just the thought of flying a helicopter would spawn a reeling, churning scene of horror in their minds. They would experience an uncontrollable anxiety attack.

On the other hand, the people in the second group (decidedly fewer in number) would be sitting on the edges of their seats, anxious for the service to end. In their minds they would already be soaring above the rooftops, practicing fancy maneuvers. They would be filled with uncontrollable anticipation!

What accounts for these different reactions? The answer is simple. The people in the second group have not only specified their abilities through experimentation and analysis, but they have also daringly put these abilities to work in a variety of new situations which have allowed them to broaden and train these abilities. As a result of experimentation and "stretching" they have seen their own competence exhibited in a variety of situations. These positive experiences have built on one another and created in these people a general sense of confidence which allows them to be genuinely excited about new challenges, like learning to fly a helicopter! Their thought processes in this situation would run something like this: "Well, I've never done anything quite like this before, but I've faced many other unique challenges, and I've had a measure of success. I've learned to concentrate, to listen carefully to instructions, and to apply myself diligently to the tasks at hand. There's no justifiable reason to fear or avoid this present adventure!"

The people in the first group, however, feel that they have every reason to avoid the "adventure." Having spent many years safe and secure in the nest of personal inactivity, they have learned to avoid all that resembles challenge or risk. They have attempted only what they know they can comfortably achieve. Since they haven't stretched their abilities, the nest of safety and security has become increasingly confining. It is like a progressive illness. Each time they choose to avoid a challenge, they make it that much easier to avoid the next one and that much harder to break out of the nest.

After the death of my father, I was very concerned about my mother. My brother and sisters and I had always viewed her as a godly but somewhat timid lady who depended heavily on our father. Then suddenly he was gone. She was 54 years of age, with good health and the possibility of a long life ahead of her. She had always been timid; now she was also brokenhearted. What would she do? How would she handle the future?

To our pleasure we watched as she learned to make wise decisions, to get involved in worthwhile community and church activities, and to intelligently handle a multitude of new and challenging responsibilities. She was willing to stretch, to grow, to learn new skills, and to meet challenges head-on. And through it all, she learned to draw more and more heavily on the strength and power offered her by the Lord.

Another woman who was willing to stretch her abilities is the business administrator at our church. Pam had a secure and lucrative job as a legal secretary for several years, but when we started Willow Creek Community Church, she felt led by God to quit her job and work for the church in whatever capacity was available. She began by working as the church receptionist and general secretary, and occassionally did light bookkeeping. As the church grew and the finances became increasingly complicated, the need for a full-time business administrator became apparent. Because of Pam's faithful and conscientious work and her apparent aptitude in this area, she was offered the position. Though she felt overwhelmed by the challenge, having a limited background in finances, she took the job and has since proven to be fully capable of efficiently organizing and maintaining a sound system of budgeting and record keeping. Watching her gain self-confidence has been extremely rewarding for me and other staff members.

The marketplace cries out for people who are willing to stretch their abilities, who are willing to accept new challenges and increased responsibilities. Most of us could go further in our endeavors than we ever dreamed possible if we took some positive steps to specify and stretch our abilities. It takes courage to do so, but it's the only way to tap the potential that rests in each one of us.

Sure we will have to face the possibility of failure; it's inherent in every positive move we make. But failure isn't so bad! I would like to shout that from the rooftops. Radical changes could take place in our lives if we realized the truth of that statement. *It's not so bad to fail!* It's OK to get our fingers dirty and our shoes scuffed and our knees bruised. All we have to do is get up, brush off the dirt, cleanse the wounds, and then try again.

Teddy Roosevelt once said, "Far better it is to dare mighty things, to win glorious triumphs, even though checkered by failure, than to take rank with those poor spirits who neither enjoy much nor suffer much, because they live in the gray twilight that knows not victory or defeat" (Lloyd Cory, *Quote Unquote*, Victor Books, 1977, p. 74).

The purpose of this chapter is not to encourage a foolhardy attitude toward risks, or to make us feel obligated to accept every challenge that comes our way. Rather, the underlying purpose is to better prepare us to accept the challenges and responsibilities that *God* sends our way, both as they relate to using our talents and gifts in the body of Christ, and being diligent workers in the secular marketplace. God has given all of us unique abilities that we should develop and use to His honor and glory.

Ten

Don't Quit—Persevere!

On October 12, 1975 we held the opening service of Willow Creek Community Church in a rented theater that smelled of stale candy and scattered popcorn. Though we started with a burst of enthusiasm and community interest, we didn't ride the crest for long. At the end of six months, the attendance had dropped, we were $20,000 in debt, the staff was exhausted and had received no salaries for six months, we were being torpedoed with criticism from several other churches, and we had received some extremely bad press. Needless to say, I was thoroughly discouraged and doubtful of my own leadership abilities.

I decided then that what we needed was a series of messages on perseverance. I remember standing up on the stage preaching up a storm about perseverance. "Don't quit!" I cried. "Don't get discouraged! Don't let setbacks defeat you!" I tried to convince myself that I was saying it for the benefit of the congregation, but inside I knew that I was really saying, "Come on, Bill, don't give up now. Sure, things look pretty bleak, and you're exhausted and discouraged and feeling the weight of criticism, but don't quit now. Don't abandon your God-given dream!"

How I thank God for His faithfulness in bringing us through those difficult days, and for helping us face the multitude of other frustrations, disappointments, and setbacks that have come along the way. Those trials and God's faithfulness have worked together to strengthen us and teach us some valuable lessons on perseverance.

111

Presto!

Think of a student who attends a new class only once and then decides to drop out because "it's obviously a demanding class" and he "doesn't want to work so hard." Imagine a young husband who, after one year of marriage, says, "I'm tired of working on this relationship. It's too frustrating. I want out." Or consider the cocky young executive who leaves the business world, dismayed because success wasn't handed to him on a silver platter.

What do these three individuals have in common? They have a common disease that's running rampant through this society. It's called the Presto Syndrome. The most telling symptom is the sufferer's unwillingness to commit himself to anything that doesn't bring easy success or a quick reward.

Though the disease has been known to be fatal, there does seem to be an antidote that has worked miraculous wonders in some cases. The antidote? Perseverance.

Perseverance is that unique quality we recognize in people who simply refuse to give up. It's the quality that helps them fight back the tears and say with firm resolution, "I refuse to accept defeat. I may face setbacks, obstacles, and trials, but total, ultimate defeat is out of the question."

Perseverance is a father and mother who wake with their hearts sick and aching because just the day before they buried their 14-year-old daughter. Though they can't escape the grief, they get up, put their clothes on, and walk out the door, willing to face the future and go on with life.

It's the student who enrolls in a class that he's failed twice before, determined not to let it get the best of him.

It's a salesman who makes the next call even though his last 15 calls have been rejected.

In its most perfect sense, perseverance is Jesus Christ carrying His own cross to His painful fate, voluntarily dying for a sinful world. Why did He keep on walking? Because He knew that was what it would take to finish the job.

I don't think that there are many superstars in this life. There are just ordinary people like you and me who do extraordinary things because they refuse to quit. They persevere.

If we fall victim to the Presto Syndrome, we'll never be anything more than ordinary people living ordinary lives. But if we learn to persevere, we can know the results and rewards of a life fully committed to reaching God-glorifying goals. We'll know what it means to honor Him with the harmony that characterizes our relationships and please Him with the quality that marks our work. We'll know what it means to establish an unquestioned level of credibility and glorify God by using fully the potential that He has placed within us.

In his epistle James tells us, "Consider it all joy, my brethren, when you encounter various trials, knowing that the testing of your faith produces endurance. And let endurance have its perfect result, that you may be perfect and complete, lacking in nothing" (1:2-4).

What does it mean to be "perfect and complete, lacking in nothing"? It means that we're fully equipped to face any hardship, any disappointment, and any pain that comes our way. How do we develop that ability? By accepting the daily trials of our lives as opportunities to practice the art of perseverance.

One of my closest friends is Joel Jager, who became a victim of crippling polio when he was only eight months old. I grew up with Joel from the time we were infants, and I watched through the years as people laughed and made fun of him. I saw him stumble and fall flat on his face the first time he removed his leg brace. I watched him learn to walk amid jeers and humiliation. I saw him struggle as the catcher for our school baseball team, occasionally diving with his face in the dirt, only to see the ball drop in the dust an inch away from his mitt. I stood by his side and watched his house burn down with every single thing that he and his family owned. I watched him ride for hours and hours on a dilapidated tractor, plowing the fields that were all that remained of the family farm. And I watched him do it all with a spirit that never failed to rebound.

The significance of this illustration is not that Joel suffered many trials; the world is filled with people who have suffered much, even more than Joel. The significance is that Joel allowed these trials to strengthen him, to make his spirit resilient. Today Joel is a member of our church staff and a constant inspiration and motivation to me because of his unique ability to persevere through anything.

Why Persevere?

I think it's obvious why a chapter on perseverance is included in a book on the Christian in the marketplace. For many people, and particularly for godly men and women who want to be more than mediocre workers, the marketplace is a frustrating and demanding world, where rewards come slowly and goals are not easily reached.

But it is not only in our workaday lives that we need to apply the lessons of perseverance. In our personal lives too we can benefit immeasurably from applying these principles.

In our church many people come back week after week just to "investigate" Christianity. They have not yet found what they need to end their search, but they're willing to keep looking. They have a faint suspicion that the Word of God has something very significant to say to them, and they're going to keep listening until they can understand what it is. For these people perseverance always brings its reward. Proverbs 8:17 says, "And those who diligently seek Me *will find Me*" (italics added).

Not only in "finding God," but also in maintaining a lifelong walk with Him, do we need perseverance. Too many people become discouraged by their inability to live "righteous" lives. They wonder why God isn't working more effectively in their lives and what happened to the "abundant life" they anticipated when they became Christians. When will everything fit together nicely so they can live happily ever after?

"For I am confident of this very thing, that He who began a good work in you will perfect it until the day of Christ Jesus" (Phil. 1:6). We needn't worry that God will abandon the work He has begun in our lives. He will live up to His side of the bargain if we'll live up to ours. And what *is* our side of the bargain? To persevere, to be willing to take one tiny step after another in a God-pleasing direction, trusting that He will ultimately perfect the work He has begun in our lives. He never promised to make us over completely in one short and easy encounter. But He does assure us that He will be faithful in helping us grow, step by step, day by day.

In our spiritual lives, and also in our interpersonal lives, we need the quality of perseverance. Because nothing is as complicated as the working of the human mind, nothing is as complex as the meeting of minds in interpersonal relationships. Because of this complexity, it's absurd to expect to develop satisfying and mutually enjoyable relationships without generous, even sacrificial, investments of time and energy. Yet many people in this society believe that they can do just that. When it doesn't work, they believe they are justified in terminating the relationship. The divorce rate clearly attests to this.

The problem, of course, is the Presto Syndrome, which spreads its ugly cancer through millions of American families each year. It has created a social climate in which it is more acceptable to deem a relationship hopeless and walk away, than it is to admit our mistakes and commit ourselves with renewed vigor to communicating, sharing, and loving.

We see this problem not just in marriages, but in friendships and work relationships too. How many once-dear friendships slide into extinction because of a disagreement that seems impossible to resolve? If only we would realize that when the spirit of perseverance is alive in us, we can hurdle almost any obstacle and withstand the "stretch" that is essential to the establishment of meaningful relationships.

We need to persevere in our spiritual lives, our interpersonal relationships, and also in the pursuit of our God-given dreams. I remember as if it were yesterday a significant experience I had when I was seven years old. In the middle of the night, my father came downstairs, woke my brother and me, and said, "Hurry up, boys. We have to go down to the produce company. I think we have a problem." When we got there, we saw a smoldering heap of charred ruins and ashes where our family-owned produce warehouse had stood just the day before.

My dad led the way, with one hand on my brother's shoulder and one hand on mine. We walked through the rubble of what he had worked for over a 30-year period. It was all ruined: the $100,000 inventory, the desks, the office equipment, the trucks that had caught fire because they were parked too close to the building.

My brother and I were devastated. When we got back in the truck, we huddled as close to Dad as we could, our eyes glassy with tears and our hearts heavy with fear. Pretty soon Dad said, "Well boys, what do you think we should do?" We mumbled that we didn't know and wondered what he was thinking. "Well," he said, "we'll rent a little house trailer and a couple trucks and we'll keep right on going." And that's exactly what we did.

Later, when I was 13, we received another late-night phone call. Again a fire had destroyed the business. But this time, as I walked through the rubble, I had no doubts about what we would do. We would rent another house trailer, buy a few trucks, and keep going.

My father's example of perseverance has encouraged me so many times in the pursuit of my own God-given dream—my ministry at Willow Creek Community Church. Periodically throughout the last six years, setbacks have threatened to undermine the efforts of all the people who have committed themselves to the ministry of this church. As I said at the beginning of this chapter, at times we even felt like quitting. But because it was a God-given dream, we didn't quit and God has honored our perseverance by pouring His ample blessing into our lives and our work.

So far I have talked about perseverance as it relates to our spiritual growth, in which all eternity hangs in the balance, our interpersonal relationships, and our God-given dreams. But beyond that, what? Does every endeavor we begin warrant our perseverance? Or are there times when it's actually better to quit?

To answer that question I need only look at my own life and admit that frequently I have gone off on wrong tangents or have begun projects that I eventually had to abandon, because they just weren't worth my time and effort, they weren't realistic challenges for me, or they simply didn't fit in with God's plan for my life. As Christians, what we do with our lives is ultimately between us and God, and it is through our communication with Him and the quiet whispers of the Holy Spirit that we should determine where to focus our energies.

We are safe, however, in establishing a few "universal goals," goals that everyone should be pursuing. As we have already said, we are all called to grow spiritually, to live in harmony with others, and to pursue our God-given dreams. We are also called to work diligently in the marketplace (including those whose marketplace is the home). We are all called to use our spiritual gifts in the body of Christ. And we are all called to take the message of God's love to the world in which we live and work. Certainly this list isn't exhaustive, but it does prove that all of us, right now, in whatever situation we find ourselves, have goals that are worthy of our perseverance. The remainder of this chapter is dedicated to helping us reach those goals.

Make Major Decisions

Some people live their entire lives without ever making one dramatic, major-league decision. Like rivers flowing downhill, they go through life constantly seeking the path of least resistance. They blindly fulfill the requirements of the public school system, go to college to please parents or peers, and ease into whatever profession grants them the easiest entrance. Then they marry and raise a family, without ever questioning the wisdom of any of these moves. In short, they spend an entire lifetime doing what is expected of them, asking no questions.

The reason that many people don't persevere in accomplishing their goals is that they haven't made a decision that involved any major consequences. I've heard it said that a decision made without risk, pain, and commitment will be pursued without passion, and I'm convinced that that's true.

Had I taken the path of least resistance in my life, I would be selling produce in our family company, I would have married a nice Dutch girl from Kalamazoo, I would be an upstanding member of the denomination that provided my early religious training, and I think I would be pursuing that life without passion. Oh, it wouldn't have been a bad life. In fact, it would have been a great life—for someone else. It just wasn't right for me. But I had to make some pretty serious decisions before I was free to break out of that expected pattern.

Before beginning to minister at my present church, I was a youth pastor at another church, and I fully expected to stay there for the rest of my life. The ministry was growing, many of the kids involved were being significantly affected for Christ, and I thoroughly enjoyed what I was doing. But then I started feeling the gentle (though firm!) nudges of the Holy Spirit to begin the adult ministry based on the principles we had developed for our high school ministry. The decision to leave the youth ministry was the most monumental decision I have ever made. There *was* risk and pain and commitment involved, but because of the magnitude and the serious ramifications of the decision, I have pursued it with a passion that I have never given to any other goal.

What about you? Have you ever made a major spiritual decision? Or are you just seeking the path of least resistance? Do you put your time in at church once a week and consider your spiritual growth complete? Are you content with being a mediocre Christian? Or would you like to line up beside those committed followers of Christ who pursue spiritual growth with a passion? It will never happen unless you make some major decisions.

What might these decisions be? If you don't attend church services, one decision might be to find a church that challenges you spiritually and to commit yourself to attending faithfully. Another might be to become more consistent in having a daily quiet time of prayer and Bible study. Another might be to obey God by using your spiritual gifts in the local body of Christ. Or to begin tithing. Or to accept God's call to be a "light" in your marketplace. The list could go on and on, but the important thing is to make a definite decision to act on the promptings you receive from the Holy Spirit and the commandments you read in God's Word.

What about your marriage? Have you made a definite decision to build a sound marriage, regardless of the effort involved? Have you made a radical commitment to your spouse? There are times in every marriage when it becomes necessary to love on the basis of decision or will alone. There are times when fidelity can prevail only because of a firm decision made at a previous time to remain faithful. There are times when the hurt is so deep and the misunderstanding so profound that only the foregone decision to persevere through *any* difficulty will enable that relationship to survive.

And what about your dream, your lifetime goal, or your career? Are you satisfied with a halfhearted performance? Are you content to let the dream remain unfulfilled? Or are you willing to make a major decision to do the very best that you can do, to actualize your potential, and to achieve your highest possible level of productivity?

Remove Mental Blocks

The night before the opening service of our church, I felt for the first time the overwhelming weight of the challenge I had accepted. Messages, counseling, challenging, encouraging, edifying, leading—the responsibility seemed awesome. I must have been crazy to accept it! How could I handle the pressure of Sunday morning and Wednesday night services, week after week, month after month, year after year? How would I do it?

I am sure that the evil one planted those thoughts in my mind in an attempt to scare me and deplete my energy before I ever got started, and he almost succeeded! Fortunately, I had had an experience many years earlier that repeatedly came to mind and helped me withstand his attack.

I was about 14 and was working on a potato farm owned and operated by the produce company. One evening my father told me to pull a flatbed semi loaded with seed potatoes into a building so that the heat from the morning sun wouldn't rot the potatoes. Well, Dad left and so did I. I was in a hurry to get to a ball game, so I decided that I would just come out early in the morning and move it.

Unfortunately, I forgot all about the truck and it sat out in the blistering sun for four days before my father noticed it. The next morning he gave me my assignment. I had to empty 500, 100-pound bags of rotten, smelling seed potatoes into a big garbage bin so that we could use the burlap bags for next year's seed potatoes.

Never has there been a job like dumping those rotten potatoes! Each time I lifted a bag, slippery black slime slid down my arms and covered my shirt and pants. The heat from the sun was unbearable and the smell of the potatoes was even worse. I started at 6 in the morning, and after 10 bags I thought I was going to have a heart attack—and I had 490 bags to go!

When my dad came by at 10 o'clock, I sat down and said, "I can't make it. I can't stand the heat and the smell. This slop is dripping all over me. A dog wouldn't do this kind of work. I've learned my lesson!"

I almost cried when he said with all the "love" and "understanding" he could muster, "Well, Bill, the way I see it you only have to do one bag at a time. Pick it up, cut it, dump it, and then lay it down. Don't look at the whole flatbed load. Just look at one bag at a time."

How tempting it is to give up on worthwhile endeavors when we look at the whole project at one time. We defeat ourselves before we ever get started. What we have to remind ourselves constantly is that we only have to grow one day at a time. We only have to love our spouses one day at a time. We only have to beat the pavement to sell our product one day at a time. We only have to face that impatient boss one day at a time.

Alcoholics Anonymous says, "Don't try to stay sober forever. Just stay sober today, and then tomorrow when it becomes today."

All we have to do is take one bag at a time. That's all, take one bag at a time, one day at a time, one session at a time, one class at a time, one step at a time. Remove your mental block. Every monster finally falls to earth and dies if we peck away at it long enough!

Remind Yourself of Your Progress

I've heard that at Weight Watchers, after a dieter has lost a sub-stantial amount of weight, he is asked to wear the clothes he wore to the first meeting so everyone can see the tangible evidence of his progress. It's so important to be able to say, "Well, I've not yet reached my goal, but I'm not where I started either."

Most of us tend to become impatient and easily frustrated when projects, jobs, goals, etc. can't be completed or reached as soon as we had anticipated. We want to see the completed picture right now, and when we can't we become discouraged. Why? Because we haven't learned to focus on our progress. We get so caught up in looking at the work we still have to do, that we forget to appreciate the work that has already been done.

We have to learn to look at our progress. When we get bogged down in our efforts, we have to look back over our shoulders and let our progress motivate us to keep going.

Remember Your Goal

Several years ago we decided to raise money to build a new church facility (we had outgrown the theater), but shortly after beginning the fund-raising project, we realized that we had taken on a stiffer challenge than we had anticipated. With interest rates and con-struction costs soaring, we were suddenly faced with a financial goal that far exceeded our projected figures. It didn't take me long to feel the weight of this financial burden, and in my weakness I began worring about the situation and doubting our decision to move ahead with the project.

Between services one Sunday morning, as I was wrestling with those feelings of fear and anxiety, I walked out into the theater lobby and noticed three little blond-haired, knobby-kneed boys huddled suspiciously in one corner. I was afraid that they might be up to no good, so I decided to check on them.

As I walked toward the corner where they were standing, I began picking up the sound of three tuneless voices singing with all the feeling they could muster. "Jesus loves me, this I know, for the Bible tells me so. Little ones to Him belong. They are weak, but He is strong."

I don't know why those little boys weren't with their class or why they had chosen to sing that song. But *their* voices, singing *those* words, had a powerful effect on me. "That's all I want," I thought. "I want to help people understand the love of God. In order to do that, we need a building where many people can join together and study and pray and grow. I can't let the pressures of our financial needs stand in the way. My goal is a worthy one. I'm not going to be defeated by this obstacle." Those little boys had helped me bring my life's goal back into focus!

What is our ultimate goal as Christians? It's to glorify God. And if that means we have to put a broken relationship back together, or be a little more diligent in our labors, or become more consistent in our faith so that we can be better missionaries to our world, then we'd better do it. Our goals are worthy ones!

Jesus the Model

Jesus was and still is the greatest example of perseverance mankind has ever known. His mission required every ounce of perseverance He had.

Though Jesus was fully God, He was also fully human, and somehow in that mystery of being both human and divine, He experienced all the temptations and pressures that we experience. But he never yielded to them. We are told in Hebrews that we have a High Priest [Jesus] who "has been tempted in all things as we are, yet without sin" (4:15). He realized the importance of His mission and so desired to glorify His Father that He refused to let anything, including the forces of hell, keep Him from reaching His goal.

At the beginning of Jesus' ministry, Satan met Him in the wilderness, showed Him all the kingdoms of the world and suggested that Jesus abandon His mission to die for His people. He was tempting Him with an easier way. "Just bow down to me," he said, "and I will give You all the kingdoms of the world. I will leave Your people alone forever. You won't have to follow Your gruesome plan of death!"

How did Jesus respond to an offer that promised to free Him from the pain and anguish that He knew His mission held for Him? He responded by holding to the Word of God. "As it is written," He said, "you shall worship the Lord your God and serve Him only" (Luke 4:8). He knew that to worship and obey God alone was the only way to fulfill His goal to free men from the chains of sin. He couldn't let the evil one tempt Him from that path.

What was it that allowed Jesus to turn away from the temptations of this world and keep His eyes on His goal? I think it was His intense single-mindedness. To be single-minded means to focus attention in one direction, on one purpose. That was the key to Jesus' resistance to Satan's attack. He never lost sight of His primary mission. Every other option that life offered paled in comparison to the calling that He had received from God. Therefore, external pressure to abandon that calling had little power to defeat Him.

But it wasn't only external pressure that Jesus had to face. When He spent His night of anguish in the Garden of Gethsemane, I don't think it was external pressure that caused Him to sweat great drops of blood (Luke 22:44). I think it was the agonizing frenzy of His own mind. I believe that the awesome weight of his impending fate drove the human element of His nature to cry for relief. Why should He shed His blood for the very people who had rejected Him? Why should He die under the immeasurable weight of human sins, when few would even acknowledge His sacrificial death?

Matthew 26:39 records His anguished plea to God and His resolute submission. "My Father, if it is possible, let this cup pass from Me; yet *not as I will, but as Thou wilt*" (italics added). Even the turmoil of His soul could not pull Him from His commitment to His goal. "As painful as it is, Father, I will do Your will."

Moments later this voluntary submission was again tested, as He experienced the disappointment of betrayal. Judas was the first to betray Him, and certainly the most deliberate, giving Him the kiss of betrayal in the Garden, but he was not the last. As Jesus' path took Him closer and closer to the cross, most of His other disciples chose to leave Him too. Fearful for their own lives, they scattered through the night, leaving Him to face His accusers alone. Surely at that point Jesus would have been justified in abandoning His goal.

But He didn't do it. He responded with that powerful quality of spirit called fortitude. Fortitude is defined as "resolute endurance; firmness of mind in meeting danger or adversity." It is that quality which allows us to close our eyes and say, "I cannot doubt in the dark what I have seen clearly in the light. I feel the mental anguish—and the weight of fear—but I know the worth, the 'rightness,' of my calling. Despite the doubts and the inner turmoil, I will keep going!"

Jesus had experienced both external pressure and internal conflict, but He had yet to know the pain of physical abuse. During the next few hours He was beaten, whipped, mocked, and spit at, and His beard was plucked. He was even forced to carry His own cross on wounded shoulders, His body so torn and weakened that He stumbled beneath the load. Finally, He was nailed to a cross, suspended naked between heaven and earth, and even then the soldiers mercilessly taunted and mocked Him.

The full meaning of the picture unfolded when Jesus cried, "My God, My God, why hast Thou forsaken Me?" (Matt. 27:46) There He was, the sinless victim, feeling painfully estranged from the Father with whom He had existed through all eternity.

In Luke 23:46 we read Jesus' last words: "Father, into Thy hands I commit My spirit." Then He died. It was finished. Jesus had succeeded in providing the way for our return into fellowship with the Father. The debt of our sin had been paid in full. Perseverance had won!

What an example Jesus leaves for us! So many times I have been strengthened by reading the Gospel accounts of His life and death. I remember one time in particular when the thought of His example helped me to persevere.

We were just weeks away from our first service at Willow Creek, and we still had no money, no facilities, and no prospective members. In order to enlist some people to join us on our opening Sunday, a few of us started knocking on doors, inviting people to visit a church that intended to minister in a positive, creative, and relevant way.

I can't begin to count the number of doors that were slammed in my face, and on one particular day in August 1975, I seemed to be batting worse than usual. I had missed lunch and dinner and I had three houses left on the last street of that day's geographical assignment. I thought, "What difference are three more houses going to make? I'm not accomplishing much anyway, and I'm sick of walking, knocking, and talking. I'm going home!"

But then I thought about Jesus and how He had persevered to the end, how He had finished the task, and I decided to keep going. I would finish the street.

When I finally reached the last house, I talked with a man and woman in their early 50s. The woman said, "Well, we're really not interested. We watch church on television on Sunday mornings." Her husband added, "That's what *she* does. I don't go to church anywhere, and I don't watch it on TV either, and I don't want to!" He was not only hostile to the idea of church, but also irate because I had interrupted the evening news.

A few months later, I received a phone call from a man whose wife had just died from a massive heart attack. "We don't go to any church," he admitted. "Could you do her funeral?" I agreed to do it.

As I was riding to the cemetery with the man, I asked him why he has asked me to do the funeral. "Well," he began, "you knocked on my door one hot August day. I didn't pay much attention to what you said, but I did remember the name of your church. When my wife died, I didn't want to walk into a funeral parlor and ask the director to say a few empty words, so I called you. Thank you for coming. This would have been an unbearable situation for me without your help."

When I went back to my office and checked the records, I realized that this man was the man who lived in the last house on the last street of my assignment on that discouraging hot day in August. I had almost passed by his house! I didn't think one more house would make a difference! I almost missed this opportunity to share the love of God with one whose heart had been opened by grief. Who would this man have called had I not made that seemingly useless initial contact with him?

That experience taught me an unforgettable lesson. We never know what is behind the next door, the next phone call, the next attempt to love, the next prayer; we just don't know. I hope these words have as much impact on your life as they've had on mine.

"Blessed is a man who perseveres under trial; for once he has been approved, he will receive the crown of life, which the Lord has promised to those who love Him" (James 1:12).

Eleven

Watch Out for the Enemy!

During the first years of my ministry, I did my best to avoid the subject of Satan. I felt uncomfortable teaching intelligent, well-adjusted, middle-class Americans about evil forces, demons, and spiritual attacks. I knew what their response would be. "Oh, here we go again, devils, goblins, ghosts, haunted houses, Ouija boards, cracks in the sidewalk, bunnies jumping out of hats. Here's a little more superstition for an already mixed-up world, a little 'old-time religion' that ought to be left to the days gone by." I knew my hearers were too sophisticated to believe in spiritual powers and too busy to worry about Satan.

Another reason that I avoided the subject was that in my own life I had never attributed my sinfulness to an external "evil power." I had always blamed my sin and disobedience on my "adventurous spirit" or my "naturally rebellious streak." I thought, "Boys will be boys! *I* know that *I* have sinned, and I'm not going to cop out by claiming that 'the devil made me do it.' I'm tough. I can take responsibility for my own sin!"

The third reason that I avoided the subject was that I had never witnessed firsthand the power of Satan. That is not to say that his power wasn't being manifested. On the contrary, his activity was all around me, wreaking its ugly havoc, but I was too naive to see it. For some reason, I never attributed the evil work and destruction going on in this world to him.

Gradually over the years, however, as I have become more

committed to loving and obeying the Lord, I have become more aware of Satan's work in my life. Why? Because I have come face-to-face with this question: If I love the Lord and want to obey Him with all my heart, why do I continue to sin?

I have come to the conclusion that I do it (in part, anyway) because there is a personal, evil force whose primary objective is to make me fall into sin. My battle is not just against the self-made thoughts of my own mind, or the evil thoughts and actions of others. It is against the "spiritual forces of wickedness," the demonic legions who carry out Satan's clever plans to turn my mind and intent from pleasing God to pursuing evil (see Eph. 6:12).

Not only have I become more aware of Satan's work in my own life, but I have also witnessed the moral ruin which he has brought on other sincere believers. I've seen godly men and women, who sometimes shamed me with their commitment to Christ, take swan dives into the depths of sin and forfeit their ministries, their marriages, and their children.

Such tragedies have awakened my mind to a passage that I memorized as a child, 1 Peter 5:8: "Be of sober spirit, be on the alert. Your adversary, the devil, prowls about like a roaring lion, seeking someone to devour."

For many years the imagery of this verse failed to move me because in my mind I pictured one of those cute little furry lions that decorates toy stores and cuddles next to children in their beds. Several years ago, however, I had the opportunity to spend four weeks on a photographic safari in eastern Africa. I remember once coming unexpectedly on the carcass of an animal that had been attacked by a lion. All that was left after the lion had finished his deadly work was a bloody heap of muscles and splintered bones. That memory helps me realize how savage Satan really is. He's no cuddly, stuffed toy. He's the enemy. He's like a real lion with real teeth who means real business, and we're his prey. The verse says that he's "seeking someone to devour," and that someone is you— and I. He takes personal delight in devouring the people who embarrass him the most—people who are devoted to Jesus Christ.

I write this chapter as one who is twice convinced, convinced first of the reality of a loving and holy God, but convinced also of the reality of a living, personal enemy who is devoted to destroying believers and unbelievers alike through his diabolical, deceitful scheming. Unfortunately, many people who read this book are probably not twice convinced. They accept the reality of a personal God, but they remain skeptical about the existence of a personal being who actually targets individual men and women for his evil attacks. It is this skepticism that gives Satan free reign to complete his evil works. He has a field day when people fail to take him seriously, for then his subtle seductions can continue undetected. I hope that you who read this chapter with skepticism will allow the Holy Spirit to open your mind to truth, so that you can become better equipped to understand and resist the attacks of Satan in your own life.

On the basis of many passages throughout Scripture, but particularly from Ezekiel 28 and Isaiah 14, we conclude that Satan was an angelic being, created holy and blameless to worship God and assist in carrying out His work in this world. Satan, however, became infatuated with his own beauty, wisdom, and power, and decided to exalt himself to a position of equality with God. He said, "I will ascend above the heights of the clouds; I will make myself like the Most High" (Isa. 14:14).

God stopped Satan's evil plot by casting him, and those who had joined forces with him, out of His presence. It is this group of rebellious schemers that makes up the "rulers, the powers, the world forces of darkness, and spiritual forces of wickedness" mentioned in Ephesians 6 and elsewhere in Scripture.

Satan's power is second only to God's. "The whole world lies in the power of the evil one" (1 John 5:19). Need we wonder why we see war, racism, unequal distribution of wealth, murder, rape, theft, divorce? The answer is that Satan is pulling the strings in the lives of the majority of the people that make up this society, and is closing their eyes to the truth of God's Word. It is Satan who attempts to keep men and women from responding to the light of the Gospel of Christ with repentant hearts. It is he who keeps them from discerning between good and evil, light and dark.

John Calvin said many years ago: "We have been forewarned that an enemy relentlessly threatens us, an enemy who is the very embodiment of a rash boldness, of military prowess, of crafty wiles, of untiring zeal and haste, of every conceivable weapon and skill known to the science of warfare. We must then bend our every effort to this goal that we should not let ourselves be overwhelmed by carelessness or faintheartedness. But on the contrary, with courage rekindled we should stand our ground in combat." With that in mind, I want to expose, in the remainder of this chapter, the tactics Satan uses to defeat us in our attempts to live godly lives in our homes, our communities, and our workplaces.

Three Hats

Satan uses a variety of methods to defeat Christians. Sometimes he capitalizes on our inherent character weaknesses, or takes advantage of our physical or emotional exhaustion. Frequently he attacks slowly, subtly undermining our efforts until eventually we give in to his pressure. At other times, he takes no chances and organizes the legions of hell to launch a blitzkrieg in an all-out attempt to permanently disqualify us from usefulness to God. All of these methods are effective, but probably his most popular method is a three-pronged attack in which he wears the hats of the tempter, the deceiver, and the accuser.

Sin begins in our minds. We think, and then we act. We see a picture in our mind, we muse over it for a while, and as it begins to take clearer focus, we face a choice: Do I act on this evil idea or do I refuse?

It is as if our mind is a blank canvas, with two painters eagerly vying for the opportunity to paint on it. The first painter is the Holy Spirit, who paints ideas that can lead us to obedient, Christlike behavior. The other painter is Satan, who paints pictures designed to lead to our disobedience and personal ruin.

Satan the Tempter works day and night to create a brilliant array of designs, some created specifically to destroy the godly men and women who are trying to honor God in the marketplace. On this battlefield of their minds is waged the war for their souls. He tempts them to let their ego-need for power rule their lives. He tempts them to take advantage of other people in their rise "to the top." He tempts men to stay late with their secretaries, knowing that their time spent together will lead to immorality. He tempts people to devote all their time to making money, even though it means the destruction of their marriages and families. Christians in the marketplace are subject to many powerful temptations, all painted artfully on screens of their minds by a crafty enemy.

Then the enemy continues his deadly attack by changing hats and becoming Satan the Deceiver. Now he begins to embellish the pictures he has painted, by offering a steady stream of promises and false justifications. "Don't worry about who you hurt on your way to the top," he says. "It's a dog-eat-dog world out there, survival of the fittest. If you have the strength to make it to the top, then you deserve it! Besides, once you get up there, you can relax and start being a 'nice guy.'

"Don't let a little dishonesty bother you. It's expected in the marketplace. You'd be a fool not to play by the accepted rules. You can't change the marketplace. You'll either have to give in or get out.

"Don't worry about spending too much time with your secretary. It's important for business associates to have 'close working relationships.' Even if you do get a little more involved than you should, it won't hurt anybody. It's all in a day's work!

"There's nothing wrong with making a lot of money. Sure, it may inconvenience your family for a while, but it'll be worth it in the end. They'll understand, or at least they should. Besides, the more money you make, the more you can contribute to your church. Who can argue with that? The Bible is filled with men who made lots of money. Think of Solomon, David, Job, Joseph of Arimathea, Matthew the tax-collector, the list is endless. God *wants* his children to be rich!"

On and on he goes. Do this and you will be happy. You deserve it. It's what you've always wanted. Give yourself a break. If someone else doesn't like it, that's their problem. Be free. Break out of your bondage. God won't care. He's a forgiving God. People won't know. If they're your true friends, they won't desert you. Try it. Just this once. You owe it to yourself.

Jesus says of Satan that "there is no truth in him. Whenever he speaks a lie, he speaks from his own nature; for *he is a liar,* and *the father of lies*" (John 8:44, italics added). Satan is nothing but a liar, but unfortunately he's an experienced liar, a master deceiver. His lies tantalize us. He paints beautiful pictures which captivate our imaginations and beckon us to turn the pictures into reality.

Satan has tempted me to quit the ministry. He has tempted me to ignore my children. He has tempted me to become arrogant about my ministry. He has tempted me to be unfaithful to my wife, insensitive to my friends, and impatient with my staff. And he has made every one of those evils sound irresistably exciting. What a deceiver he is! What a liar!

Do you remember Satan's first lie? He approached Eve in the Garden of Eden and said (according to my paraphrase), "Hey, Eve, why don't you taste the fruit on the tree in the middle of the garden? It's beautiful and juicy. It's the choicest fruit in the garden." As the Tempter, he began to paint the picture in her mind, and when she hesitated, he put on the hat of the Deceiver. "No, you won't die. Oh sure, God *said* you would die, but He didn't *mean* it. On the contrary, you will become like Him, knowing good and evil. Why would God create such beautiful fruit if He didn't intend for you to eat it? Perhaps He's just waiting to see if you have the courage to try it. Don't you realize what it would be like to have all knowledge and discernment? You won't die, Eve. You're the crown of God's creation. Would He let you die?"

But Eve did die. The consequences of her sin were real. God is a loving God, but He is also a Holy God. When we believe Satan's lies and yield to sin, we have to pay the price of that sin. We have to reap the rewards of our disobedience.

And how Satan enjoys that! How it pleases him to see us broken by shame, by fear, by despair and alienation. He loves it! But even then he doesn't consider his task complete. Oh, no, he has yet to claim the hat of the Accuser and point the penetrating finger of guilt.

Now, when we're on our faces, broken and humiliated, begging for God's forgiveness, he begins his cruelest plot. He plants his weighted foot in the middle of our back and says, "You phony. Do you think that God will ever forgive you for what you've done? Don't you realize that you're no longer worthy of His love? Do you think He can still use you, after what you've done? Do you think you will ever be of value to the kingdom of God? You might as well face the facts. You've had it! You're through!"

Satan the Accuser is brutal, utterly heartless. And those of us who fall prey to his accusations become immobilized and paranoid. Even when we begin to sense the definite beginnings of God's forgiveness, Satan comes back and says, "That forgiveness won't last. You better ask again and again and again." If we listen, we become crippled, never able to get up and move on in our walk with the Lord.

But I know what some of you are saying. "That would never

happen to me. Satan has never had any 'big victories' in my life, and he never will. I'm happily married. I work hard, but I don't go overboard. I don't ignore the kids. I don't step on people to make it to the top. I'm honest, I'm consistent. I go to church. I read my Bible. I pray. I tithe and even give offerings. I watch my language. I help my neighbor. I'm basically a pretty good guy. This chapter is fine for some people, but I really don't need it."

To you who say that I offer hearty applause. I'm glad that your strong moral constitution and your sensitive conscience keep you on your toes. I'm thrilled that your relationship with Christ is genuine and that you have the power to resist Satan's overt attacks. But I think it's important that you understand one very important fact. *Satan does not admit defeat. He never gives up his goal. He only changes tactics!*

An Alternate Plan

If Satan can't devour us by acting as Tempter, Deceiver, and Accuser, he takes a new line of attack. He tries to *neutralize* our faith. He does this by convincing sincere young believers that their new and boundless enthusiasm is nothing more than a manifestation of spiritual adolescence which *will* and *should* fade with age. He likewise convinces more mature believers that they should demonstrate their spiritual maturity by living serious, predictable, semi-sedated Christian lives that attest to their "quiet consistency." In short, he tries to dupe you and me into "mellowing out" and "settling in" to a powerless, watered-down, neutralized Christian existence.

Chad Walsh writes: "Millions of Christians live in a sentimental haze of vague piety with soft organ music trembling in the lovely light from stained glass windows. Their religion is a pleasant thing of emotional quivers, divorced from the will, divorced from the intellect and demanding little except lip service to a few harmless platitudes. I suspect that Satan has called off his attempt to convert people to agnosticism. After all, if a man travels far enough away from Christianity, he is liable to see it in perspective and decide that it is true. It is much safer, from Satan's point of view, to vaccinate a man with a mild case of Christianity so as to protect him from the real disease" (*Early Christians of the Twenty-first Century*, Greenwood Press, page 11).

Satan doesn't have to devour us. He has only to ease us into a comfortable, pseudo-Christian mind-set, thereby rendering us innocuous, spiritually impotent, and pathetically useless to God's kingdom.

In Revelation we read about the church of Laodicea that was comfortable and harmlessly inactive. There was no ugly division in the church, no gross immorality or serious misinterpretation of truth. Today it would probably be called a "nice friendly church." But to God it was a despicable church, a church filled with "mellowed out," neutralized believers. He said, "I know your deeds, that you are neither cold nor hot; I would that you were cold or hot. So because you are lukewarm, and neither hot nor cold, I will spit you out of My mouth" (3:15-16).

Why was God so upset by these neutralized Christians who were neither hot nor cold? Because they made a mockery of Christ's sacrificial death. When God gave His only begotten Son, blameless and pure, to be nailed to a cross for our sins, He gave us only two options. Either we bow our knees to Him in humble adoration and commit ourselves to honoring Him, or we thumb our noses at Him. There is no middle ground.

Imagine a professional football team that's two touchdowns behind at the half. The coach is feeling the pressure, he's got a chalkboard full of ideas, and he has every intention of going into the locker room and rallying the troops for a come-from-behind victory. But let's suppose that a few of the players say, "Oh, sure, we'll go out there and play the game, but right now we want to take a little break, maybe go down and visit the cheerleaders, have a hot dog and a few beers, sign a few autographs."

How do you think the other players would respond? I think they'd probably say, "Hey, boys, if you want to get off this team, fine. We'll be glad to find someone to take your place. Or if you want to get in here and dedicate yourselves to winning this game, that's OK too. But if you think you can walk around like you don't have a care in the world, and then still consider yourself to be on this team, *you are wrong!* You either knock yourself out to win this game, or you get off the team!"

Like the committed players on this team, God does not appreciate a careless, disinterested attitude. In Malachi 1:6 we read His words to the Israelites who had become lax in their devotion. "A son honors his father, and a servant his master. Then if I am a Father, where is My honor? And if I am a Master, where is My respect?"

"What's wrong with you people?" God asks. "You call me 'Father,' but you give Me no respect. You're all talk, and no action."

In verses 7 and 8, He continues, "You are presenting defiled food upon My altar . . . when you present the lame and sick, it is not evil?"

According to the Jewish religion, the sacrificial lamb was a very important part of worship, symbolic of the Israelites' wholehearted devotion to God. Therefore, only perfect animals, without sickness or deformity, were to be used for the sacrifice. Yet here we see the priests, the highest religious leaders, calmly offering God blemished animals obviously believing that He wouldn't mind their spoiled leftovers.

But God continued, "Why not offer it to your governor? Would he be pleased with you? Or would he receive you kindly?" To us He would say, "What would your boss think if all you gave him were your leftover time and your leftover talents? Or what about the IRS? Would they appreciate your leftover treasures? How would they respond to a note that said, 'Sorry, I know I'm a little short on this year's taxes, but you don't mind, do you?'" We wouldn't think of offering earthly authorities anything less than what they demand, but how frequently we fail to take God's demands seriously.

And what is God's demand? Our total devotion. Our undivided allegiance. He wants a holy lamb or He wants no lamb.

What about our time? Do we honor Him with the time we devote to our families? Are we conscientious in the way we use our time at work? Do we spend enough time in prayer and personal Bible study? Do we take time to worship God and thank Him for what He's done in our lives? Or do we give Him the leftovers? The fleeting thoughts and the empty prayers? Do we blame our negligent attitudes toward Him on the economy? Do we justify them by saying, "Well, you know it's getting tougher and tougher to be a success. It's taking more and more time. I don't enjoy working overtime, but it's not an option anymore; it's necessary." Is that your justification for being too busy to honor God and too tired to think of spiritual growth?

What about our talents? Do we honor God with the excellence of our work? Have we made every effort to tap the potential that God has placed within us? Many of you who read this book are multi-gifted and multi-talented, but who benefits from those gifts and talents? The body of Christ? Or just you?

What about our treasures? I think the underlying reason the priests refused to offer the unblemished animals to the Lord was that they brought a better price in the marketplace. It was all a matter of dollars. What about us? Are we willing to honor God with our tithe, or do we give Him a dollar here and a dollar there, whatever is leftover? Some who read this book have used their talents to build fortunes on this earth. Could not those same talents be used to profit the work of the Lord?

Are you one of those who leaves evangelism to the so-called "professional Christian workers"? Have you already forgotten the call that God gave to Jonah and that He gives to us today? Are you unwilling to accept your responsibility to be a "light" to your marketplace and a missionary to your world? Are you neutralized?

My father was an extremely sharp manager and shrewd businessman. The produce company, which most people erroneously believed to be his major business concern, was just one of the many projects in which he was involved. He actually made as much money by buying failing companies which he nurtured into productivity and then sold for a sizable profit. He did this repeatedly by enlisting new management for the companies, reorganizing the bookkeeping and accounting procedures, and then putting out the time and energy required to build up the accounts. He had the vision necessary to see the potential in the ailing companies, and the leadership skills necessary to fulfill that potential. That's what led to his success.

It wasn't until the last two years of his life, however, that he began applying those skills to the building of the kingdom of God. During that time he began to envision a wilderness camp where the kids and adults of our church could get away from the fast-paced life to which they were accustomed, and enjoy a quiet environment that would be more conducive to their spiritual growth. He saw that dream, and then he provided the land, the financial resources, and the leadership skills to bring that dream to reality. During the last summer of his life, he had the joy of seeing the first group of campers "initiate" Camp Paradise.

The Saturday before he died, as we stood in my garage, he said,

"You know, Bill, if it weren't for you kids and the camp, my life wouldn't amount to much at all. I'm just so thankful that I finally found out what is really worth working for."

Greater Is He That Is in You

Satan attempts to devour us, and if that fails, he attempts to neutralize us. As Christians in a secular marketplace teeming with Satan's tempting lies, have we any hope? Can we possibly succeed in living godly lives in such a world?

First John 4:4 says, "Greater is He who is in you than he who is in the world." Satan is powerful, but his power is without a doubt second to the power of God. On our own we would surely be helpless victims, but we are not on our own. We have within us the Holy Spirit of God who is greater than any foe.

God knows our limits. He will never allow us to be tempted beyond our ability to endure. If we keep ourselves alert to Satan's deception by focusing our minds on the truth of God's Word, we will be able to resist his evil plots and see God's alternative, "the way of escape" (see 1 Cor. 10:13).

Yes, we have an enemy, but we also have the power, through Christ, to conquer him.

What was God's response to the deceived, neutralized Christians described in Revelation 3? Did He tell them that they were hopeless? That they were unfit to be His servants? That they must forever remain Satan's fools?

On the contrary, we read that He begged them to recognize Satan's lies and repent of their sinful attitudes. He challenged them to break out of their patterns of halfhearted devotion and honor Him with their undivided love.

And that is the same challenge He gives today. The church does not take the message of the Gospel to the marketplace. Only individual men and women who are committed and obedient to Jesus Christ can do that. That's why Satan focuses his attacks on them. If He can undermine their devotion to God he can keep the message of God's redeeming love imprisoned within the stone walls of half-filled sanctuaries.

Twelve

God Has a Robe for You

One of Satan's chief goals is to blind our minds to the truths of God's Word. If he can cloud our minds with confusion and misunderstanding, he can keep us from responding in obedience to the various "calls" that God gives to believers.

In this book we have talked about just a few of these calls. We have learned that God calls us to labor diligently in the marketplace. He calls us to be witnesses of the reality of the living Christ, to be missionaries to our world. He calls us to be honest and pure and to work with excellence. He calls us to live in harmony with other people. He calls us to be wise consumers and godly investors. He calls us to develop our abilities and our spiritual gifts. He calls us to persevere in using those skills to honor Him.

But before He calls us to do any of these things, He calls us to do something else that is far more important. He calls us to establish personal, life-changing relationships with Him. He calls us to become permanent members of His family, so that we can walk in daily fellowship with Him throughout this life and on into eternity. This is by far the most significant call of all. It is the foundation on which a God-honoring lifestyle can be built.

Is it any wonder, then, that this is where Satan most often aims his attacks? If he can keep us from understanding the fundamental truth of the Christian faith, he can prevent us from living obedient, God-pleasing lives here on earth and he can also keep us from securing eternal life with the Lord in heaven.

Passing the Test

For many years Satan was successful in blocking my understanding of what it meant to be a Christian. He did it by convincing me that achieving "good standing" with God was just like achieving anything else. If I worked hard enough at it, I was sure to succeed. If I conscientiously used my God-given abilities, and persevered in living a moral life, I would pass the test. I would ultimately succeed in gaining God's favor, establishing a meaningful relationship with Him, and securing my future heavenly destination.

The big question for me was: How could I be sure that I was being "moral enough"? How good did I have to be to pass the test? How much service did I have to give Him? What was the standard for which I should aim? When would I know, beyond a shadow of a doubt, that I had done enough to earn my way to heaven?

I finally decided that the only way I could be sure to earn God's favor was to offer Him the ultimate act of devotion: I would become a missionary. Surely, if I sacrificed the luxuries and conveniences of civilized society and committed myself to spreading the Word of God to primitive areas of the world, then God would grant me entrance to heaven.

I took a very pragmatic approach to the situation. I determined my goal (to please God), I decided how I could best achieve that goal (by becoming a missionary), and then I began to take the necessary steps. I talked my father into sending me on an eight-week-trip to South America, so that I could visit various mission stations and decide where to give my future service, the service that would assure my way to heaven.

What an incredible trip! It began in the country of Panama, where I took a banana boat as far as it could go, then switched to a dugout canoe, and finally traveled for miles on foot, visiting missionaries in numerous jungle tribes and villages. I watched, I listened, and I pondered. I had an important decision to make with eternity hanging in the balance.

Words that Changed My Life

I have no doubt that I would be serving God in a remote jungle today, had I not met a godly missionary whose words changed my life.

"Bill," he said, "don't you realize that you can't earn your way into a relationship with God? You can't buy heaven. You can't merit God's favor. No amount of good works you compile can help you meet His standards, or help you pass the test."

Those words wouldn't leave me; they haunted me continually. As I began my journey home, I started to read the Bible. Again and again, I read the same message. "For by grace you have been saved through faith; and that not of yourselves, it is the gift of God; *not as a result of works, that no one should boast*" (Eph. 2:8-9, italics added).

Not as a result of works, the Bible said. *You can't earn it. You can't buy it. You can't merit it. Your good works don't count*.

Gradually, I began to understand what that wise missionary had said. Slowly the truth of Scripture began to make sense to me. I finally realized that in developing my plan to earn God's favor, I had ignored the very important fact that *our God is a Holy God*. His standard is absolute perfection. His test is the test of absolute holiness. That's why my good works and my outward acts of devotion could do nothing to help me gain my entrance into heaven. However good they might have been, they still fell far short of perfection. They were still stained and spotted with sin, rendering me unworthy of entrance into God's holy kingdom.

Envision, if you will, the kingdom of God as a magnificent building in which dwells the Father, the King of kings. Outside the door to the kingdom are huddled the masses of humanity who seek entrance to the great hall. They are unable to see beyond the door, but were they able, they would see the blazing light of God's presence, the light which symbolizes the essential characteristic of His nature: holiness. It is this light that fills the hall, leaving no room for darkness, not even a shadow of sin nor a hint of impurity. "God is light," says the Apostle John, "and in Him there is no darkness at all" (1 John 1:5).

It is for this reason that the masses remain huddled beyond the door. Their lifelong efforts to gain God's favor appear as nothing more than dark spots on tattered garments. Such darkness has no place in God's kingdom of light.

God's Standards

Tragically, many people in this world do not understand what God's holiness means. They mistakenly believe that God's standards are just the same as ours, and are therefore attainable through human efforts. But such is not the case. The Bible teaches that it is against God's perfect and holy standard that we will be judged, and found sadly lacking.

A simple illustration may help to clarify this. The month before we moved into our new church building, the architects and the general contractor scheduled a final inspection for the auditorium ceiling. Because the ceiling height reaches 45 feet in some places, the ceiling work had to be done on hydraulically operated lifts which were so large that the builders had to leave one outside wall of the auditorium unfinished so they would be able to remove the machines from the building. Consequently, this inspection was very important. Once the machines were removed and the wall completed, it would be impossible to do additional ceiling work.

In anticipation of the inspection, I spent many days in the auditorium, identifying defects in workmanship and making sure that they were corrected. On the day of the inspection, I met the architects and contractor at the building, expecting to be able to give them permission to remove the lifts. However, our church staff person in charge of programming, lighting, and sound had other intentions. Arriving at the auditorium early, he had focused two high-intensity flood lights on the ceiling, and by the time we arrived he was busy jotting down all the little defects that had gone unnoticed under normal room lighting.

The instant the contractor saw the lights, he sent an electrician downstairs to pop the circuit that fed them. With evident indignation, he said, "This inspection is to be conducted in normal room light. *No workmanship* can withstand the test of high–intensity lights!"

Do you see the point? The enemy, Satan, makes every attempt to lull us into believing that we will never stand in the blazing floodlight of God's holiness. He tries to convince us that we will only be judged by human standards, and that our defects will not be evident.

But, again, the straight teaching of the Word of God says otherwise. It says that we will stand in the floodlight of God's holiness, with every defect of attitude or action exposed. Every little white lie shows up as an ugly stain on our clothes. Every little act of selfishness leaves an embarrassing spot. Every immoral thought or deed appears as one more obvious flaw in the fabric of our lives. And no

man or woman is powerful enough, wealthy enough, or manipula-
tive enough to coerce God into pulling the plug on the spotlight. It
can't be done.

Divine Dilemma

It is at this point that we begin to see the divine dilemma that has
captivated the minds of theologians for hundred of years. On one
hand, we have a God whose absolute purity prevents Him from
tolerating sin in any amount or any form. On the other hand, we
have a God who is hopelessly in love with sinful men and women.
On the one hand, He is compelled by His holiness to cast them from
His presence. On the other hand, He is compelled by His love to
clutch them to His breast. What can He do?

We find the answer to that question in the Book of Revelation,
which is the written description of the Apostle John's God-given
vision of heaven. In Revelation 7:13-17 we read, "And one of the
elders answers, saying to me [John], 'These who are clothed in the
white robes, who are they, and from where have they come?' And I
said to him, 'My lord, you know.' And he said to me, 'These are the
ones who come out of the Great Tribulation, and they have washed
their robes and made them white in the blood of the Lamb. For this
reason, they are before the throne of God; and they serve Him day
and night in His temple; and He who sits on the throne shall spread
His tabernacle over them. They shall hunger no more, neither thirst
anymore; neither shall the sun beat down on them, nor any heat; for
the Lamb in the center of the throne shall be their Shepherd, and
shall guide them to springs of the water of life; and God shall wipe
every tear from their eyes.'"

Who are those who will stand in the presence of God? Who will
serve Him joyfully night and day? Who will hunger and thirst no
more? Who will have every tear wiped from their eyes? They are
those who have had their tattered, sin-stained robes *washed white
in the blood of Christ*. In these few words is found the heart of the
Christian message.

In order to get a clearer picture of this truth, let's once again
picture the kingdom of God as the great hall which houses the light
of God's presence. Imagine that you are walking toward the door of
the kingdom, hoping against hope that you will be allowed to enter.
As you approach, you see that the door is haloed by an unearthly

glow. When you get closer, however, you realize that the "halo" is really the escaping rays of light that refuse to be contained behind the wooden door. So brilliant is their light, that even these scattered rays have the awesome power to expose the previously unseen. As you stand spellbound by their power, you begin to notice that your garments appear soiled and lightly stained. You wonder why you didn't notice that before, and then suddenly realize that the light stains are becoming darker and darker. Could it be that the colors are actually deepening right before your eyes? Or is the light opening your eyes to realities that you simply had not noticed before? Yes, that's it! Along life's journey your robe had become ragged and black with sin, but you just hadn't been able to see it, or perhaps you hadn't looked.

A Gleaming White Robe

As you stand there, contemplating your inexcusable blindness, you begin to see the hopelessness of your plight. The kingdom you see before you is the kingdom of holiness and the light you ponder is the penetrating light of God's presence. Surely, no one whose robes are stained and spotted with sin will be permitted inside this kingdom of perfection.

In utter despair you turn to leave, but just then you hear steps behind you. Glancing back over your shoulder, you are amazed to see the sinless Christ, brilliantly robed in gleaming white, smiling.

"Would you like to enter the kingdom?" He asks.

"Yes," you reply. "I long to be a part of God's family, to live with Him forever. But I am unfit. His kingdom is the kingdom of perfect light, and in that light my darkness is exposed. I cannot enter."

Once again He speaks. "But do you not *desire* to enter?"

"Yes, oh, yes," you cry in frustration. "But in these rags?"

"No, My child. My Father would not accept those rags. But I will exchange your soiled robe for Mine of gleaming white. Here, take it, put it on. Then you can go into the kingdom."

You attempt to speak, but you find no words. You can't even bear the thought of the Sinless One wearing your rags. You stand silent, in disbelief.

Finally He speaks. "It's the only way, My child. Only My robe is pure enough to withstand the intensity of My Father's light. Take it, and enter."

Your heart heavy with remorse, you begin to remove your filthy rags. You don't look up, but soon you feel His tender touch as He places His robe on your body. Then He says, with gentle confidence, "Now you're ready. Go inside and stand before My Father." Before you walk through the open door, you turn and watch Him walk slowly away, burdened under the weight of your soiled robe.

As soon as you enter the room, you understand why there is only one robe worthy to be worn there. Each corner of the great hall is bathed in the light of purity. The walls, the floor, and the ceiling all glow with the radiance of God's holiness. And then you see *Him*, the King of kings, on His throne, and you are melted by His loving smile.

"The robe," He says. "I've seen it before. Where did you get it?"

Surely He knows your answer. Could He think that you would dare claim it as your own or say that you earned it? Too well He knows the condition of the rags you wore as you approached the kingdom.

You whisper the only word that will satisfy His question. "Jesus." And then His smile widens as He says, "Welcome home, My child. This is where you belong. Come, join the celebration! One whom I have loved and called has made the exchange and now stands unblemished in My presence!"

The picture painted in these last few pages stirs my heart to thanksgiving! Why? Because I know the condition of my clothing. I know that in them I would be forever unable to stand in God's presence. And yet, because of Christ's sacrificial death, I shall stand in God's presence!

You see, when the sinless Son of God hung on a cross between two thieves, He accepted the entire weight of human sin. Picture the throngs of humanity stopping at the cross of Christ and throwing on His shoulders all their filthy rags. One by one they come, each adding weight to His already-overwhelming burden. When He cries, "My God, My God, why have You forsaken Me?" it is nothing more than a rhetorical question. He *knows* why God has forsaken Him. In taking on our sin, He has made Himself unacceptable to the holiness of His Father. He has given God no choice but to remove His presence from Him.

So it was that Jesus took on Himself the alienation from God which we deserve, and which we would experience through all eternity, were it not for His voluntary death. Yes, He took with Him to the cross the accumulated rags of human sin and freed us to accept His robe of purest white. But what exactly does that mean? When do we place the robe on our shoulders? Do we wait until we stand in the shadow of heaven's gate?

No. We will have no time, after death, to contemplate our plight. It is here, today, in this life that we must decide to respond in love and faith to Jesus' accomplished work of salvation. It is here, through the revealed truth of Scripture, that He meets us and offers us His robe of redemption.

So Few Accept

The ultimate tragedy of the universe is that so few people accept the robe. Because of Satan's clever lies, most people remain blind to the true condition of their clothing. They wander around in normal room light, looking at one another and saying, "Who needs a Saviour? We're really not so bad!" They have no understanding of the total incompatibility of a Holy God and a sinful man.

Others refuse the robe because they are deceived into thinking that somehow, in the end, they will be able to solve their sin problem themselves. Rugged individualists, they refuse to accept the fact that there is *anything* they can't accomplish on their own. Unfortunately, many successful businessmen and women fit in this category. They conveniently close their minds to a discussion such as this, because it forces them to admit their limitations, something they cannot afford to do. Instead, they cling to their delusions that somehow, sometime they will solve the problem on their own.

But they can't do it. Their stubbornness will only lead them to a godless eternity. In Acts 4:12 the Apostle Paul says of Jesus, "And there is salvation in no one else; for there is no other name under heaven that has been given among men, by which we must be saved." Jesus is the *only* answer to our sin problem. He is the only One who can cleanse us and make us worthy to stand in the presence of God.

Has Satan been attempting to cloud your mind to the simplicity of this truth? If so, now is the time to recognize his deception and respond to Christ on the basis of the biblical truths presented in this chapter.

Begin by acknowledging your sin. Look at your tattered clothing

144 / Christians in the Marketplace

in the light of God's holiness. Isaiah 64:6 says, "For all of us have become like one who is unclean, and all our righteous deeds are like a filthy garment." As you look at the reality of your sin, don't yield to the temptation to compare yourself to others. Such comparisons are meaningless. In the blazing light of God's holiness we are *all* stained with sin. Romans 3:23 says, "For all have sinned and fall short of the glory of God."

The next step is to acknowledge what the Bible says about Christ's sacrificial death; that in dying He took on Himself the shame and weight of our sin and experienced the complete and terrible alienation from God that we deserve. If you sincerely acknowledge that truth, your inevitable response will be one of gratitude, a gratitude that compels you to ask His forgiveness for committing the sin that nailed Him to the cross.

The final step is the exchange itself. With humility and broken-ness, you allow Him to place the perfect robe on your shoulders, trusting that it, and nothing else, will give you the privilege of walking boldly into the presence of God.

One of the unique beauties of the Christian faith is that it is not just a faith for the future, to assure us of God's presence in the hereafter. It is also a faith for today. Yes. Today we can walk, by prayer, into the presence of God and say, "Here I am, a sinner who has been cleansed and robed by the Saviour. On the merits of this robe, I call myself a Christian. Thank You for allowing me to be a permanent member of Your family!"

As men and women who live in a world darkened by sin, we are called first to respond personally to this message of God's love and then to share it with others. I believe the church must be viewed as more than simply a refuge *from* the workplace. It must also be viewed as a place to refuel so that we can make an impact for Christ *in* the workplace.

Jesus cherished the time He spent in prayer and fellowship with His followers. But He also demonstrated a passion for ministering in the marketplace. It is my prayer that you will seek to follow the example of the One who gave His life for you.